Continuing Education

THE ESSENTIALS

Greg Marsello, Editor

Published by LERN Books, a division of
Learning Resources Network (LERN)
P.O. Box 9
River Falls, Wisconsin 54022
U.S.A.

Phone: 800-678-5376 (US and Canada)
E-mail: *info@lern.org*
URL: *www.lern.org*

Additional copies of THE ESSENTIALS are available, usually without cost, from LERN. Contact us for details.

Manufactured in the United States of America

5   4   3   2

Library of Congress Cataloging in Publication Data
  Continuing Education: The Essentials

ISBN 1-57722-036-6

Contents

Chapter 1
Introduction

Continuing education is one of the most rewarding fields of endeavor and work. It is essential to the improvement of the quality of life for all individuals. It is necessary for the success of business, government and employers. It is the primary delivery mechanism for lifelong learning. It enhances the sense of community. It is central to the improvement of society in the 21st century.

Continuing education is also critical to the mission and future of institutions that host continuing education programs. Continuing education provides unique contributions to help position your institution for continued success as we transition from the last century into the new knowledge society and information age of the 21st century.

THE ESSENTIALS is designed for anyone working in or associated with the field of continuing education, including:

Leaders

Continuing education CEOs will find the most important research and leadership practices for positioning your continuing education program for success in the changing marketplace of the 21st century. The book also serves as an independent objective way to verify the best management strategies in addressing an increasingly competitive external environment. And it is a handy guidebook for the training of continuing education staff and personnel to reduce risks and avoid failures.

Central administrators in institutions will receive the required information necessary for the oversight of continuing education units. Decision makers now have a resource for understanding how continuing education is a distinct and highly skilled, sophisticated and specialized area of work. And institutional leaders will have additional evidence to demonstrate how continuing education is critical to the mission of the institution, providing unique contributions to help position the institution for greater prosperity and service in the 21st century.

Professional Staff

Professional staff will get a checklist of the most important strategies, techniques and practices in improving continuing education operations, marketing and new program development. Every professional staff member working in the field of continuing education should have a working knowledge of the information contained in this book, especially the benchmarks and ratios for success. With this book, professional staff can improve execution, productivity and results, avoid the most common mistakes made in continuing education, and learn new ways to best use valuable and limited staff time.

New Staff

New staff members will find a unique resource for getting acquainted and up to speed quickly and effectively in their new positions. Continuing education is a different and specialized occupation, with unique skills and requirements. New staff will get the best introduction to the fundamental concepts and every-day processes that make continuing education programs work effectively and productively.

Everyone reading this book will find guideposts pointing to more advanced information. THE ESSENTIALS is a condensation of the fundamentals in continuing education. This book is intended as a beginning, a start, into the increasingly sophisticated knowledge areas of the field of continuing education.

LERN specializes in advanced cutting-edge research in continuing education practice for continuing education programs ranging from hundreds of thousands in income to $25 million or more. LERN provides answers and solutions to continuing education programs pursuing greater success.

Our professional consulting and training staff is the largest and most expert in the world in the field of continuing education. Contact us with your needs. For further resources, a bibliography and list of services for you and your program is provided at the end of the book.

Chapter 2
Overview of the Field

Continuing education has always been important to society and individuals alike, but in the 21st century the new knowledge economy will make continuing education even more central to success for individuals, employers, professions, communities and society as a whole. At the same time, continuing education has become a very sophisticated, competitive, skilled and specialized business. This combination of *mission* (service to society) and *money* (the requirement to be financially self sufficient) make continuing education a unique, exciting and rewarding profession.

Continuing education in North America (Canada and the United States) differs somewhat from other countries around the world in that North America has a diverse provider base, with almost every and any type of organization participating in offering some kind of continuing education. It is that richness of offerings and choice for the learner that makes continuing education in North America innovative and of high quality.

There are a variety of providers in the field right now. Traditional non-profit institutions are major players. They include:

- Community colleges and technical institutes serving both the local community and area-wide audiences with continuing education.
- Universities and four-year colleges serving local, state and national audiences with continuing education.
- Public schools serving local communities with community education.

- Park and recreation departments serving local communities with recreation programming.
- Associations at the state and national level serving occupations, professions and interest areas with association education.
- Hospitals, museums, libraries, and other non-profits.

Joining these non-profit institutions is an increasing number of for-profits. They include:
- Businesses specializing in continuing education and training for one or more audiences.
- Corporations offering customer education.
- Shops and stores offering "boutique" courses for a niche market.
- Consultants and trainers providing specialized courses for a niche market.
- Online providers scanning the globe with general and specific online offerings.

Continuing education is usually thought of as organized educational offerings for adults beyond formal schooling in which there is a teacher and one or more learners.

Much continuing education is open to anyone in the public, other continuing education is available to anyone but of greater interest to someone in a particular occupation or profession.

Other continuing education is developed on contract for a specific client, company, or organization and is closed to the general public.

Almost all courses offered without credit are considered continuing education. Some credit and degree programs, such as night classes, evening college, summer courses, graduate degrees, non-traditional degrees, and online courses may be considered continuing education by the college or university offering them.

Continuing education is generally NOT:
- Literacy, adult basic education, GED or high school degree completion.
- Full-time degree programs for students of traditional age, 18-22.
- On-the-job training or in-house company training.

Lifelong learning is a much broader term which encompasses just about any kind of learning throughout life.

Within continuing education there are some distinctions in offerings, with some differences in benchmarks, procedures, and ratios for success among them. The two major broad areas of continuing education are open enrollment courses and contract training.

Open enrollment continuing education has two important different kinds of offerings. They are:

Professional continuing education

Work-related offerings, targeted to workers and employers, with brochures often mailed to an individual at the place of work. Professional development, professional studies, continuing professional education, and education are some of the various terms used.

Community programming

Avocational and leisure offerings, with some business and professional development courses included, targeted to individuals, with brochures often mailed to an individual at the place of residence. Community education, adult education, general interest classes, and leisure education are some of the various terms used.

Contract training

In addition to open enrollment courses and offerings, continuing education may also include contract training — education developed on contract for a specific client, company, or organization and closed to the general public. Customized education, work force development, training and in-house or on-site education are some of the various terms used. Contract training has led to consulting, a growing area of contract training for continuing education.

For administrators of continuing education, each of these major areas of continuing education has some variation in successful operations, professional staff skills, ratios for success, benchmarks and specialized skills.

Within open enrollment offerings, a wide variety of formats are engaged, including:
- One-night-a-week classes
- One-night-only classes
- Weekend classes
- All-day seminars
- Multiple-day seminars and Institutes
- Conferences
- Certificate programs
- Trips and tours
- Special events and festivals
- Lectures
- Tutoring and mentoring
- Consulting
- Online courses

Other formats are emerging, evolving and being created frequently to respond to the needs of customers.

Chapter 3
History & Philosophy
of Continuing Education

The Philosophy of Continuing Education

The philosophy behind continuing education is often understated, implicit, and rarely discussed or debated. Yet throughout the history of North America, three philosophical tenets about learning and teaching have evolved and become accepted by most if not all providers of continuing education. Understanding these three philosophical tenets is essential.

1. The responsibility for learning rests not only with the continuing education program administration, but also with the teacher and the participants.

Continuing education promotes self-directed learning. Much of continuing education is voluntary, not mandatory. And almost all education authorities and professors say that continuing education is more successful when it is undertaken voluntarily and enthusiastically by a learner, rather than being mandated to a reluctant learner.

Continuing educators often act as a linking mechanism between teachers and other subject matter experts and the participants, leaving the subject matter content to the teacher or instructor, and the evaluation of whether the course was satisfactory up to the participants.

While continuing education providers and administrators take responsibility in the administration and offering of courses and activities, sometimes even guaranteeing them, responsibility for successful teaching and learning is shared with teachers and the participants.

One ramification of this notion of shared responsibility is the concept of self-directed learning. Continuing education places a good part of the responsibility for learning on the learner. This brings up the recurring argument about whether people know what is good for them, and continuing education as a field predominantly comes down on the side of "yes," or at least that people should know what is good for them. Learners ought to be able to distinguish a good class from a poor one. Learners ought to be able to judge whether they are learning, whether they have developed a competency in the content of the class, and whether the instructor is able to help them learn.

2. Anyone can learn.

While this philosophical concept is widely accepted today, it has not always been the case. Before 1970, it was believed that you could not "teach an old dog new tricks," as the saying went. Many people also believed that a traditional formal education was enough to last throughout one's life.

Today it is commonly believed that anyone can learn, and that learning should continue throughout one's lifetime, with the term lifelong learning having evolved and gained popularity. And yet continuing educators often are at the forefront of extending the notion that anyone can learn to new frontiers, breaking down other barriers and outmoded beliefs.

One ramification of this philosophical tenet is the notion that learning is good in and of itself, having both internal rewards as well as external rewards. Not all learning has to be for credit or a degree in order to be valuable.

Another ramification is that if anyone can learn, and all individuals are in some way different from each other, then individuals must necessarily then learn differently. Today continuing educators are exploring ways in which to help individuals learn in a variety of ways.

And yet another ramification is the notion that we each can, and should, learn throughout our lifetime. Continuing education is unique and essential in that it not only embraces but carries out and executes the notion of lifelong learning. Without continuing education, lifelong learners would be without one of their primary ways to continue learning.

Continuing educators understand that lifelong learning extends one's actual life, keeping the brain and body active longer in life. Continuing educators understand that avocational and leisure learning keeps the brain active for workers and employees who then can acquire new work skills much faster. Continuing educators understand that lifelong learning is positive not only for the individual, but for businesses and community development and the economy and for society in general. When an individual engages in lifelong learning, everyone benefits.

3. Anyone can teach.

The notion that anyone can teach, and can teach anything, was also considered educational heresy at one time. Today continuing educators understand that people who are doing something are most often the best teachers of that 'something.'

Continuing educators also understand that new subject matter is being created every day. Continuing educators understand that an unlimited offering of courses and subjects is far preferable for all concerned than a limited offering, and that the marketplace of participants is the best judge of what can and should be offered in almost all circumstances.

There is an unlimited number of topics and specialties that adults want to learn about today, and the only way to meet that need is to encourage learners to be teachers as well. In fact, it is a repeatedly proven concept that the best way to learn something is to teach it. Thus, the interplay between teaching and learning is very positive and beneficial.

At one time this "right to teach" any subject was challenged by traditional gatekeepers. But always the freedom to learn in a democratic society was tied to the freedom to teach. Continuing educators have behaved responsibly in this regard, and so have almost all teachers and learners. There have been almost no instances of irresponsibility when it comes to teaching various subjects and topics in a democratic society.

Other ideas about the role of continuing education
In addition to these three basic concepts about continuing education, there are other ideas about the purpose and role of continuing education in society. Some of them are stated here.

Informal structure. That continuing education is supposed to remain flexible, responsive to the marketplace, providing interaction among people as well as subject matter, and that social interaction among participants is a positive side effect that actually enhances the learning.

The community is a learning environment. The community is a learning environment which provides a rich array of resources for learning and teaching. Some of the resources are not always visible, and continuing educators play a role in discovering some of those resources and making them available to the public.

Linking knowledge and action. That continuing education is one way in which knowledge can be linked to action, and that community development, economic development, social progress, and other positive societal action and individual action comes from continuing education. There is also the belief that individual self development, behavior change, and growth can, should and does stem from continuing education.

Process is as valuable as content. Many continuing educators believe that the process of learning, engagement, teaching and sharing is as valuable as the actual content of a class. The process of learning, of learning how to learn, engages the brain and allows us as individuals to later acquire other knowledge when needed in a much faster and more productive manner.

Responsiveness to the community. Whether the community is local and geographic in nature, or dispersed and targeted by occupation or interest area, that continuing education is, and is supposed to be, responsive to the individual needs of the community it is serving.

Education creates social change. Since the beginnings of adult education in the history of North America, continuing education has often led to positive social change in society, and continuing education can and should be a catalyst for social change, offering innovative and alternative ways of thinking so that society can move forward.

A Short History of Continuing Education

The history of Continuing Education has evolved both from institutions and from adult educations. For much of the history of North America, continuing education activities were called adult education.

Adult education developed very differently from formal schooling. Historically, adult education programs have arisen to meet specific needs, not as part of an overall general design of education for the country.

There is a rich tradition of adult education throughout the history of our country. During Colonial times in America, apprenticeships were a common way for young men and women to learn a trade. Although organized to some degree, an apprenticeship was essentially an agreement between two people. The apprentice would agree to work for his or her "teacher" for a given length of time and in return would be trained in an occupational skill. Benjamin Franklin is sometimes referred to as the father of adult education in this country. In 1727 he formed in Philadelphia a weekly discussion group called the Junto. Subscription libraries, the predecessors of today's free public libraries, were started in colonial times. In those days, people paid a subscription for the privilege of using a library, with the fees going to purchase new books. The primary education institution of those times was the church.

Between the Revolutionary War and the Civil War, other adult education movements arose. The lyceum movement which flourished between 1826 and 1839 was a popular one. It was started by Josiah Holbrook and comprised a series of lectures and town forums offered in circuit fashion throughout the small towns of New England and later extended to other parts of the country. Public libraries and museums started during this time, and mechanics' institutes were instrumental in providing training — the Cooper Union and the Lowell Institute being two famous ones. Such voluntary associations as the YMCA blossomed, leading de Tocqueville, a French commentator of the time to note that America was a land of volunteer organizations.

The time between the Civil War and World War I was a transitional period, with the country moving from an agricultural economy to an industrial one and people moving from rural settings to increasingly urban ones. Cooperative Extension was started during this time, as were a multitude of correspondence courses. Perhaps the most intriguing movement of the time was the Chautauqua movement. It was started on the shores of Lake Chautauqua in New York State as a residential summer church school. Soon it became popularized, and its range of study broadened to include cultural, artistic, political, and even scientific endeavors. With speakers, plays, music, and demonstrations, summer learners were both entertained and informed. In due time, other Chautauquas were established, and then traveling Chautauquas, using circus tents, were sent throughout the East and Midwest. Millions of people would attend a Chautauqua in its heyday, listening to the great speakers of the time, outstanding musicians and vocalists, and other performer-educators. Although the movement died in the mid-1920s, its spontaneous birth, fresh and innovative style and orientation to the general public have made it an exciting example of adult learning in our history.

Since the 1920s, much adult education was institutionalized —
in labor unions, churches, Cooperative Extension, the military, business and industry. But much of it still arises spontaneously at
different times to meet local needs, sometimes startling professional educators. The moonlight schools of Kentucky were started
by a woman who saw the need to teach reading to adults. Being a
public school teacher, she opened up her school at night so adults
could attend. They were called moonlight schools because the adults
could only come on moonlit nights when they could see their way
to the school. The Highlander Folk School in Tennessee, started in
1927 by Myles Horton, remains to this day a testament to the
craving that adults have for linking learning with their own social
condition. Highlander has provided a place where poor mountain
people, blacks, labor leaders, coal miners, and others could come
and learn from each other. Some of the recent great social movements have been spurred on by unique adult learning centers.

In the 1960s civil rights leaders engaged in adult education
activities to help African Americans understand their voting rights
and to encourage them to vote. These unstructured activities were
called Freedom Schools. After college students participated in one
such effort in the south in the summer of 1964, the college students
took the idea of Freedom Schools back to their campuses and turned
it into Free Universities.

The first Free University started in the fall of 1964 at the University of California at Berkeley. The concept, educational heresy
at the time, was that anyone could teach, anyone could learn, and
any subject could be offered. Courses were ungraded and offered
without credit, and became enormously popular. Free universities
spread to over 300 campuses, and then were started as independent
entities in communities and cities all across North America.

The free university model, both in terms of philosophy and in
terms of structure, practice and marketing, became so successful
with the general public that traditional institutions began to adopt
and expand their own course offerings using the free university model.

Many institutions had been offering courses before. But beginning in the 1970s the numbers of offerings, the broadening scope

and variety of those courses, and number of institutions offering courses began to explode. Over the next thirty years the number of people participating in such courses would triple.

Colleges and universities expanded their non-credit offerings, calling them continuing education. Public schools expanded their offerings to adults, calling them community education. Parks and recreation departments expanded their class offerings, calling them recreation programs. Associations expanded their educational offerings to members, calling them association education. Museums, hospitals, vocational technical institutes, libraries and other non-profit organizations also began or expanded their course offerings. Some for-profit companies, local businesses, shops and stores also began offering courses to customers and potential customers. In all, one central feature of continuing education in North America is the rich diversity in providers and subjects offered to the public and targeted audiences.

The term "continuing education" became popular in the 1970s, replacing "adult education" as the most common term. In 1964, Congress in the United States passed the Adult Education Act providing funds and support for adult basic education and high school degree completion for adults. From then on, the term adult education became confused with adult basic education.

Continuing education implies a continuing of one's education beyond college. From the 1970s to today, studies show those most likely to participate in continuing education are people with undergraduate degrees or some college.

Continuing education today continues to undergo change, adapting to the ever-changing marketplace and needs of the public. Given that the 21st century is seeing an information or knowledge economy replace the industrial economy of the last century, continuing education is likely to be even more important to individuals and society in this century than ever before.

Chapter 4
Learning & Teaching

How Adults Learn

As an administrator of a continuing education program, you not only work with teachers and instructors. You also are a teacher yourself. Administrators and staff in continuing education thus should know these essentials about how adults learn.

The adult's mental learning state is not a blank chalkboard on which you, the teacher, can write as you wish. Neither is the adult learner's head an empty pail for you to fill with your knowledge and ideas. The adult learner's chalkboard already has many messages on it, and his mental pail is almost full already. Your job as teacher is not to fill a *tabula rasa*, but to help your participants reorganize their own thoughts and skills. A prerequisite to helping adults learn is to understand how they learn.

As complex human beings, we bring to the learning situation a combined set of emotional, physical, mental, and social characteristics that make each one of us unique. The way to approach this diversity in learners is with variety in your teaching. To do that, it is best to understand some of the characteristics of adults.

Emotional Characteristics

Adults' emotional states are inextricably tied up in their ability to learn. To learn, an adult must be emotionally comfortable with the learning situation. Indeed, some educators have gone so far as to equate a good emotional state with learning. Says J. Roby Kidd in *How Adults Learn*, "Feelings are not just aids or inhibitors to learning; the goal of learning and of emotional development are parallel and sometimes identical and can probably be most conveniently stated as self-realization and self-mastery."[1]

Throughout the ages, one's emotional state has always been manipulated to try to induce learning, but somehow the attempt to produce positive feelings became distorted in the mistaken belief that greater learning would occur if one produced negative feelings of pain, fear, or anxiety.

The dunce cap, a sign of humiliation, was not originally intended to be so. Instead, the cone-shaped headgear was believed to have magical powers, just as some contemporaries believe the similar pyramid shape has unknown powers. Putting the cap on one who had missed a question or needed help was not a punishment, but was believed to help that person learn. Over the years the symbolism changed from a positive helping gesture to a sign of humiliation and ignorance.

Unfortunately, vestiges of the punishment principle either consciously or unconsciously are present in even the most enlightened classes. Learning can be inhibited by frowns and other gestures.

In helping a person learn, the teacher must be able to help create a positive emotional climate, and the key to that state is one's *self-image*.

Although most adults come to class mentally ready to learn, at the same time, they may be inhibited from learning by a poor self-image. That poor self-concept may not be correct, may not be rational, but nevertheless exists in many people. It comes from various sources.

A shy person may feel unable to participate to meet the expectations of others in the class. A manager who has been turned down for several promotions may feel trapped in a dead-end job and doubt the value of learning anything. A housewife who has stayed at home with children for many years may feel she is not current or informed enough to converse on an adult level again. Someone who has been out of school for several decades may feel incapable of studying anymore, and may fear being left far behind the other students. The causes of a less-than-positive self-image are many. They stem from natural feelings about inadequacy and growing older, and some are induced artificially by society.

Physical Characteristics

Abraham Lincoln may have been able to read at night by firelight, and children may have learned in straight-backed wooden desks in drafty log cabin schools, but today's adults can detect and be influenced by the slightest changes in comfort. Adults are more attuned to comfortable surroundings, more sensitive to discomfort.

Make sure your setting is comfortable, neither too warm nor too cold. Older people chill more easily, and your sense of warmth may not coincide with those in your group. In a small crowded room, your participants will become hot and stuffy sitting next to each other sooner than you will. Ask your participants to tell you if they are uncomfortable.

All adults in your class, even the younger ones, are declining physically. Everyone is aging, even those who refuse to admit it. Our physical state affects our capacity to learn. Physique and intelligence are related because our bodies influence how and whether we can learn.

To compensate for visual difficulties of learners of all ages, think carefully about how you can make words, charts, objects, even yourself, clear to all your participants.

Set up your room so that no one has to look directly into sunlight. Make sure there is enough overhead lighting. If you use a flip chart, use large letters when writing on it. Seat people so they can see each other. Participants will engage in discussion and learn more from each other if they can see each other.

Just as important as seeing well is hearing well. Inability to hear well, either because of one's own capability or because of the setting, can make learners feel insecure, less intelligent, isolated, and far less willing to participate.

In preparing your class, think about how you can ensure that every participant will hear you. Try to select a room that is reasonably free of outside street noises, or noises from other rooms in the same building. Listen for any interference from heating sources, air conditioning, coffee pots, and any other systems or appliances in the room.

Design your space so that you can always be heard by your participants, and so that they can hear each other. If you have a large class, experiment to see if a microphone helps or hinders. Speak in clear, loud, and distinct tones. Don't talk to your group with your back turned to them while you are concentrating on something else, like setting up some projection equipment. Ask as often as you need to whether people in the back can hear you. When others in the class are talking, make sure they are facing the majority of the class. Ask people to stand up if necessary. Repeat questions from the group so everyone can hear them.

Mental Characteristics

Although adults may come to the learning situation with bodies that are not always in prime shape, the story is different for their mental attitudes. Mentally, adults are eager to learn — otherwise they would not be there.

Several aspects of adult learning mentality relate to your helping them to learn: a readiness to learn, problem orientation, and time perspective.

A readiness to learn. Adults for the most part will come to your class ready to learn. Almost all adult learning is voluntary these days, and even societal coercion, such as peer pressure, does not seem to affect adult learners. They attend because they want to.

Part of that readiness may be a natural growth process in which "true learning" — self-study, personal inquiry, or self-directed learning — is more welcome after one's formal schooling or education ends. Even the sixteenth century master of self-study, Montaigne, wrote about his education, "At thirteen... I had completed my course, and in truth, without any benefit that I can now take into account."[2] Whether their experiences in school were beneficial or not so positive, adults want to view their adult learning experiences as separate from more formal school, and will approach them differently. This may be because adults are not only ready to learn but need to learn.

Problem orientation. Education for children is often subject-centered, concentrating on various disciplines like philosophy and science, and the abstract as well as the practical. Adult learning, on the other hand, is more problem-centered. Adults want to learn to solve or address a particular problem, and are more satisfied with their learning if it applies to everyday experiences, is practical, or is current.

Adults are oriented toward problem solving because they are faced with certain developmental tasks stemming from the roles they assume, or want to assume, in their families, work, and society. These tasks and roles demand a good deal of adjustment, accomplishment and learning. Although society pushes few adults into the classroom, it certainly creates enough needs and wants to encourage adults to perform their best in various roles and life stages.

Time perspective. Another and related impetus for problem orientation in adult learning is that an adult's time perspective is different from that of a child. For a child, time, both past and future, is a vast quantity. A year ago is a long time. And the future is endless. Increasingly, as one becomes older, time becomes less expendable and more limited. The future is not so endless after all, and the past blurs a little so that ten years wasn't all that long ago. As time becomes more limited, it becomes more important. In the learning situation, adults prefer what can be learned today or in the near future to what can be learned over a longer period of time. The adult's interest in solving problems within their older time perspective makes adults more concerned with specific narrow topics of relevance than broad, generalized or abstract subjects.

A readiness to learn, problem orientation, and specific time perspective contribute to an internal motivation to learn.

The time and problem orientations do not imply that everything adults want to learn is so immediate as fixing the plumbing. Many different kinds of issues, thoughts, and ideas may constitute a timely problem. For one person, finding out whether beauty lies in a museum painting or in a mountaintop view may constitute a legitimate learning problem. For another person, determining how the ancient philosophers combined work with study may be an equally immediate problem.

Social Characteristics

The most important social characteristic of the adult learner is an abundance and variety of *experiences*. This aspect alone makes teaching adults different from teaching children or youth.

Your participants will be coming from different backgrounds, occupations, types of upbringing, ethnic heritages, and parts of town. Each one will have a different mix of experiences and previously formed perceptions when entering your class. Some of these perceptions are about school group interactions, and the subject.

School. Even if you are not working in a school-like atmosphere, structured learning situations are inevitably associated with previous schooling. For many people, their formal schooling was less than successful. Many adults received low grades in school and have some stigma attached to that period of time. Others may have outwardly done well in school, but inwardly felt the experience was boring or a waste of time. Generally speaking, it is best to reduce the number of associations with formal schooling in your references, style, and approach to your subject. When teaching those with unfavorable school experiences, it is wise not to repeat those mannerisms and actions which may remind your participants of their past situations. The imprint of our schooling is still on all of us, and if those memories are not good, it is best not to revive them.

Group interactions. Your class is just one kind of group in which adults participate. Some will come with positive expectations about interacting in a group; some will not. Some will come wanting to be leaders in the group; others will have already decided before the class starts to be passive or take a minimal role in group participation. Some will see the group as an opportunity to display talent and knowledge while others will see it as a possible threat to exposing their lack of talent and knowledge.

The subject. Every adult coming to your class will have some perception about the subject to be discussed. Some will have a degree of proficiency in the topic; others will have been acquainted more superficially. Some will have had a negative encounter with the topic, or gained some misinformation. Others will have thought about it from a distance, but come with curiosity and some ideas not based on reality, but on what others have said or done.

Social psychologist Gardner Murphy says that adults, contrary to common assumption, are not able to detach themselves emotionally from the subject at hand. "The adult has not fewer but more emotional associations with factual material than do children, although we usually assume that he has less," he says.[3]

Working with your participants' experiences is perhaps your most rewarding challenge. These varied and copious experiences need to be handled on two levels. First, you as a teacher need to deal with the backgrounds your participants bring to class. If someone has a negative image of schooling, you may have to help that person see this situation as different from past schooling. If a person in the group has gained some misinformation about the subject, you will need to clarify the misinformation. If some of your participants automatically shy away from participating in a group, you may want to try to draw them out or structure exercises to give them as much interaction as your over-eager students have.

On another level, you have an abundant resource at hand in the past experiences of class members. Each has some event, skill, idea, or knowledge worth sharing with the rest of the group. As Sharon Merridan and Rosemary Cafarella note, "Life experience functions in several ways... Adults call upon their past experiences in the formulation of learning activities, as well as serving as one another's resources in a learning event."[4] You can tap into the variety in backgrounds to illustrate your points, to encourage discussion, to stimulate peer teaching, to gain new knowledge yourself. It is this wealth in your participants that makes teaching adults so exciting and rewarding. Drawing on your participants' experiences can make the class an exciting and new interaction every time you teach; to ignore the past is to miss out on something valuable and special.

Motivation to Learn

The total of one's mental, emotional, physical and social states determines a person's motivation to learn. Much attention throughout history has been paid to how to motivate people. Generals have tried to motivate troops, supervisors have tried to motivate workers, salespeople have tried to motivate themselves, staffs have tried to motivate boards of directors, and boards of directors have tried to motivate staffs.

The quest for motivation has led to much thought on the subject as well. Those writing about the power of positive thinking can stay on the best seller list for weeks or even years, and those speaking about it can fill halls with rallies on motivation.

Most authorities on adult learning advocate encouraging self-directed learning. For example, author Laurent Daloz says, "We teachers sometimes speak of pushing our students to higher stages of development. We want the best for them after all, and need to know that we have made a difference in their lives — an important difference. To push a person to change is about as effective in the long run as trying to push a chain uphill. People develop best under their own power."[5] As a teacher, you will doubtless be confronted by people with a range of motivations. How much time you want to spend stimulating motivation is up to you.

This author's experience is that almost all people want to learn. A given person may not want to learn a specific subject in a specific way at a specific time, but that person is nevertheless motivated to learn provided there is a subject of interest engaged with his or her own learning style.

Most adult learning experts agree that while motivation comes from the learner, responsibility for motivation to learn rests not only with the learner, but also with the teacher and program administration.

You as a teacher can help or hinder another person's attempts to learn. By failing to recognize limits, by ignoring or even constructing barriers, by not understanding how a person learns, you can be a negative influence on someone's learning. By facilitating learning and helping your participants, you can be a positive influence.

Attributes of a Good Teacher

We can describe the most commonly accepted characteristics of what makes a teacher of adults effective. But the descriptions will be general, and denote attitudes and basic skills. It may even leave you a bit unsatisfied; and that is simply because there is no one *way* to teach adults.

This author, like most of you, can recall having learned something on a snowy evening around a cabin fireplace while chatting with another person, and having learned just as much while sitting in a straight-backed high school desk in a classroom with a former West Point instructor lecturing. You will undoubtedly remember, as we list some of the favorable characteristics of adult teachers, equally outstanding teachers who didn't have a sense of humor, didn't care at all about the students or listen intently, and yet they excelled in teaching.

Nevertheless, it helps to talk about the kind of teacher people respond to most of the time. Even if you cannot develop every skill to the fullest, if you are sincere about becoming a good teacher, you probably will succeed. One of the chief characteristics of adult learners is that they appreciate and sympathize with someone who is trying.

Educator Frank C. Pearce describes the ideal teacher of adults as "people-centered, more interested in people than things, more interested in individuality than conformity, more interested in finding solutions than in following rules. The teacher must have understanding, flexibility, patience, humor, practicality, creativity and preparation."

One must meet three requirements before being able to teach adults:
- a basic competence in the subject,
- a desire to share one's knowledge,
- a wish to help adults learn.[6]

Basic competence. The first requirement has intimidated many potentially good teachers of adults because they have mistaken a basic competence for exceptional competence. Although the more one knows about a subject, the more one can share, most people underrate their competence rather than overrate it. If you have a basic competence and are honest about your skills and experience in describing the course, by all means teach.

Desire to share one's knowledge. The second requirement is essential. Someone with a basic subject competence will likely be a far better teacher with a desire to share it, than would be a subject expert without a desire to share it.

A wish to help adults learn. The third requirement is not only critical, but becoming more important than simply a subject expertise. Helping adults learn is such an essential teaching skill that it should occupy more of your time and attention than the subject material.

In evaluating classes, the problem most students point to *least* is the teacher's knowledge of the subject. Most student complaints are not about the teacher's knowledge of the subject but the teacher's ability to share that knowledge.

Furthermore, teachers of adults acquire much of their competence by doing and experience. Credentials play a minor part in the teacher's credibility and the student's interest in one's teaching ability. The old saying, "He who can, does; he who cannot, teaches," just doesn't hold true for teaching adults. In most adult learning, it is the person who can who does the teaching.

Chapter 5
The Official Dictionary of Continuing Education

A standardized set of definitions and terms
used in programming and marketing classes for adults

Active Classes/Events: This is the number of classes/events actually held in a session or year.

Annual: A twelve-month period. There is no standard year for class programming. Some programs measure a "school year" from September through August, while others measure a "calendar year" from January through December.

Annual Enrollments/Registrations: Annual enrollments/registrations is the total number of registrations for a program for a twelve-month period. Do not include registrations or refunded registrations for canceled classes, only those who registered for active classes.

Average Class/Event Fee: The average class/event fee is the average fee charged to participants for a single class/event. It is important in analysis of income and in forecasting enrollment projections. The best way to determine the average class/event fee is to divide the total registration income for a session or year by the total number of registrations for that time period. This is the method LERN recommends to calculate this statistic. For example, if your class program had $50,000 in registration income for a year and had 2,000 enrollments for that time period, the average class/event fee would be $25.

Average Income: Sometimes called the average income per person, this is the dollar figure the average participant pays in a particular session or year. To determine this figure, divide the total registration income for a session or year by the number of participants for that time period. For example, if a class program's registration income for a session is $20,000 from 1,000 registrations coming from 400 participants, the average income per participant is $50. (Not to be confused with the average income per registration, in this case, $20.)

Average Income: Sometimes called average income per registration enrollment, this is the same as the average class/event fee. See "Average Class/Event Fee."

Average Participants per Class/Event: The average participants per class/event figure is the average number of participants taking any given class/event. It is important in analyzing enrollments and projecting future enrollments and registration income.

To determine the average participants per class/event, divide the number of registrations per session or year by the number of active classes/events held. Do not include either canceled classes/events or registrations for canceled classes/events in the figure. For example, if a class/event program has 5,000 enrollments for a year and offered 417 classes, of which 333 were active classes/events actually held, then the average participants per class/event would be 5,000 divided by 333, or 15.

Auxiliary Income: Self-generated income that is not registration income. For example, auxiliary income could come from the sale of T-shirts, books, tapes, or other fee-for-service income.

Break-Even Point for a Class/Event: The point at which an individual class' income equals the expenses for that class/event. The break-even point for a class/event is figured as the registration income for that class/event less all expenses, including teacher fee, room rental, promotion and indirect costs. To determine the promotion costs for an individual class/event, divide your total promotion costs (brochure, brochure distribution, advertising, etc.) for the session by the number of classes/events offered. To determine the indirect costs for an individual class/event, divide your indirect costs (staffing, office rent, etc.) for a session by the number of classes/events offered.

Brochure: A publication published every session listing all of the classes/events offered, with registration information and form. Many programs also refer to a flyer that promotes only a single class/event as a "brochure."

Brochures Distributed: An important statistic in analyzing promotion. This is the number of brochures actually distributed, not the number of brochures printed. Brochures distributed is measured per session. Only if the term is followed by "per year" would the figure indicate the number of brochures distributed annually.

"Distributed" includes brochures mailed, put out in stores and shops (even if some of them were not actually taken), inserted in newspapers, given to teachers and others, and distributed from the class program's office. The only brochures not included in this figure are brochures printed and kept bundled or otherwise not distributed. It also does not include any advertisements or other promotions not involving the actual brochure.

Brochure:Participant Ratio: This is the number of brochures it takes to get one registration. It is determined by dividing the number of brochures distributed by the number of registrations for a given session or year. It is an important statistic in analyzing promotion, increasing the number of brochures distributed, and forecasting future enrollment. For example, if a class program distributes 100,000 brochures for a session and receives 2,000 registrations, the brochure:participant ratio is 50:1. This statistic can also be expressed inversely as a response rate. The brochure:participant ratio is commonly used by class programs distributing brochures through shops and stores and newspaper inserts as opposed to strictly direct mail.

Canceled Class/Event: A class/event which was offered and promoted in the brochure, but for whatever reason was not actually held. Reasons include lack of sufficient registrations, a teacher becoming ill or otherwise not able to teach, meeting space not obtained, and so on.

Catalog: Same as brochure. See "Brochure."

Class: A class is a learning activity in which there is a teacher and one or more participants. A class may meet one night, meet several times, meet all day, or be a tour if learning is involved. It is a generic term covering all learning activities that can be measured.

Class/Event Cancellation Rate: The class/event cancellation rate is the percentage of classes/events canceled in any given session due to insufficient registrations and any other factors, such as the teacher not showing up. To determine this figure, divide all the classes/events canceled (if two sections of the same class/event topic are canceled count it as two classes/events) by all of the classes/events offered in the session.

Class/Event Fee: The price charged to a participant for a particular class/event or course. Sometimes called a "course fee."

Classes/Events Offered: This is the number of classes/events listed in the brochure or promoted in some way. It includes both active classes/events (those actually held) and canceled classes/events (those that were promoted or advertised but not held). The number of classes/events in a session is all of the separate groups meeting for that session. If one topic or course title has three sections, that is three classes/events. Each individual class/event or section is counted once, regardless of how many times it meets during the session. For example, a class/event meeting six times is counted as one class/event.

Class Program: This is a generic term developed by the Learning Resources Network (LERN) to designate any organization offering classes for adults. A class program may be an entire organization or part of a larger institution. It is an organizational unit which programs and markets classes for adults, registers participants, and evaluates the classes.

Classes/Events per Participant: Sometimes called number of classes/events per person, this is the average number of classes/events each participant takes. To determine this figure, divide the number of registrations for a session or year by the number of participants for that time period. The number will be 1.0 or greater. It is usually between 1.0 and 2.0.

Course: Same as class. See "Class."

Drop-Out Rate: The drop-out rate is the percentage of participants who register for classes/events but are not in attendance at the final meeting. To determine this figure, divide the total number of participants attending the final class/event meetings (if one person is taking two classes/events count each class/event attendance) by your total number of registrations for the session.

Enrollments: An enrollment is the same as a registration. See "Registration" for definition.

Facilitator: Same as teacher. See "Teacher."

Financially Self-Sufficient: This is a class program in which self-generated income, such as registration income and income from brochure advertising, or other fees for services, equals or exceeds expenses without any subsidies included in income. See also "Subsidies." Expenses includes indirect expenses, such as supplies, share of office rent and utilities, staff salaries and fringe benefits. A totally financially self-sufficient program is one in which self-generated income exceeds all expenses, including indirect costs and/or overhead.

Flyer: Some programs refer to a brochure which promotes only one event or class as a flyer. This is not a common usage among all class programs.

Income: Income is registration income plus any other income, such as subsidies, institutional reimbursements, grants, or other monies coming to the program. In a totally financially self-sufficient program, registration income and income are usually the same.

Independent Contractor: A legal term used by some class programs to designate teachers as independent agents and therefore not employees of the class program. In order to maintain this distinction, the class program usually also maintains that the responsibility for learning and teaching in the classes/events are the responsibility of the teacher and participants, not the class program itself.

Instructor: Same as teacher. See "Teacher."

Materials Fees: Materials fees are charges to participants in addition to the normal class or course fee and a registration fee. The money is totally to cover materials such as paper, books, art supplies or whatever supplies are necessary for the class. Materials fees are most often paid directly to the teacher or some entity other than the class program.

No-Show Rate: This is the percentage of participants who register for one or more classes/events but do not attend the first class/event or any subsequent class/event. To determine this figure, divide the number of no-show registrations by the total number of registrations.

Participant: A participant is a person taking one or more classes/events. If one person takes three classes/events, that is one participant. If two people take a class/event, that is two participants.

Participants per Session: This is the number of participants or people who register for a particular session. It is NOT the same as the number of registrations per session. For example, if each and every one of 1,000 people registers for two classes/events for a particular session, the number of registrations for that session is 2,000, but the number of participants per session is 1,000.

People: Same as participant. See "Participant."

Production: Production expenses include teacher or instructor costs, classroom rental, handouts, cost of sending out evaluations, and any materials costs. Production expenses are a variable expense.

Productivity Rating: A measurement developed by LERN to establish a baseline ratio from which a class program can measure changes in its staff productivity. The rating is somewhat arbitrary, just like the Dow Jones Average, and is useful primarily in comparison to previous years. To find the productivity rating of a program, multiply the class program's surplus percentage for the last fiscal year by ten, and then subtract the staffing expenses percentage.

Promotion: Promotion expenses are those direct expenses involved in trying to get participants to register. They include the brochure or catalog typesetting; printing; brochure distribution; advertisements for classes/events; billboards, and other similar promotions. Not included in promotion expenses are staffing costs, handouts for class participants, or office rent, among others. Promotion is often discussed as a percentage of registration income. To determine your promotion expenses as a percentage, divide your total dollar promotion expenses by your total registration income. These numbers can be either for a session or annually. Annually is statistically a better time period to use.

Registration: One person taking one class/event or activity. If one person takes two classes/events, that is two registrations. If two people take a class/events, that is two registrations.

Registration Fee: A fee charged in addition to the class fee to cover costs of registering a participant. It is charged only once per participant, regardless of how many classes/events the participant registers for.

Registration Income: Registration income is the total dollars of income generated from participant fees. These fees include class or course fees plus any registration fee added to the class or course fee. It does not include any materials fees if those fees are paid to the teacher or some other entity.
Registration income is usually calculated by session and by annual registration income.

Registrations per Session: The number of registrations for a given session, not including registrations for canceled classes/events. It does include registrations for which monies were refunded for active classes/events. An average number of registrations per session would be the actual registrations for the class program's last year divided by the number of sessions offered in that year.

Registrations per Year: Same as "Annual Enrollments."

Refund: A refund is money given back to a participant. Different programs have different policies regarding refunds, and there is no standard refund policy. Refunds include money returned to participants due to illness, any other inability, or dissatisfaction with the class/event. Refunds also include money returned to participants whose classes/events were canceled due to insufficient registrations.

Refund Rate: The refund rate is the percentage of income returned to participants who registered for a class/event that actually took place. It does not include returned money to participants whose classes/events were canceled due to insufficient registrations. If a participant registered for an active class/event but did not pay, that is counted as income and as a refund. To determine the refund rate, divide the total dollars returned to participants in active classes/events by the total dollars of registration fees for that session.

Repeat Rate: The percentage of participants in a given class session who also registered for the previous session. For example, a repeat rate of 65% means that 65% of your participants from last session also registered for your current session.

Response Rate: This is the average response rate a class program receives in registrations from mailing out its brochure or catalog. For example, if a class program mails 100,000 brochures and receives 2,000 registrations from those brochures, the response rate is 2.0%. Response rate can also be expressed inversely as a brochure:participant ratio. Response rates are most commonly used by class programs using direct mail as the primary promotion method of distributing brochures.

Self-Generated Income: Any income that comes from fees generated by the program for services offered by the program. Self-generated income includes registration income and auxiliary income. It does NOT include subsidies.

Semester: Same as session. See "Session."

Session: A session is a period of time, usually one to four months, during which classes/events take place. Almost all sessions have a separate brochure or catalog describing the classes/events for that particular session. A session is NOT the number of classes/events offered, and it is NOT the number of times a class/event meets during a given session or term.

Sessions: This is the number of discrete and separate per year sessions offered in one year. The range in sessions per year is 1 to 12, with the average being 4.

Staff Expenses: Staff expenses are salaries and benefits for full and part-time staff employed by the class program. This does NOT include training costs for staff, staff travel, or other staff related expenses. The figure also does NOT include teacher expenses. Staff expenses are often expressed as a percentage of income. To determine the staff expenses percentage, divide the dollar amount of staff expenses for a year by the dollar amount of income.

Students: Same as participant. See "Participant."

Subsidies: Any monies not coming from participants or other direct fees for services. Subsidies include tuition reimbursement from state agencies, monies from a central institutional office, or staff salaries paid for by any means other than from registration income. A subsidy also includes covering of indirect or in-kind services, such as office space, telephones, heat and other utilities, office equipment, and furniture. To determine the percentage to which your program is subsidized, divide your subsidy income by your total income.

Surplus: Surplus is the amount of money left over at the end of the fiscal year. Surplus as a dollar amount is figured as the difference between income and total expenses. To be a financially self-sufficient class program, registration income and other self-generated monies must exceed total expenses. For example, a class program receiving $50,000 in subsidies, and spending $80,000 in expenses for that fiscal year is NOT financially self-sufficient. Expenses before surplus should include staffing and any indirect or overhead costs such as a share of office rent, utilities, equipment and so on.

Surplus Percentage: Surplus is often expressed as a percentage of income. To determine the surplus percent, divide the total dollar surplus amount by the total income for the fiscal year.

Teacher: A teacher is anyone who leads a class/event, sharing knowledge and promoting learning among the participants.

Teacher Expenses: Money paid directly to teachers for their services of teaching. Does not include materials fees, training costs, a teacher newsletter or other costs of recognizing teachers. Teacher expenses are often stated as a percentage of registration income.

Term: Same as session. See "Session."

Year: Same as annual. See "Annual."

Chapter 6
Finances & Budgeting

The Only Financial Format To Use

Your institution's way of keeping finances is based on fund accounting, or being accountable for how the funds are spent. Fund accounting is inadequate for continuing education. By continuing to use your institution's system, you will never be able to determine if you are making money, what is making money, what the problem is, and where the solutions lie.

That is why we recommend keeping two sets of books, both accurate, of course. Keep the set of books which your institution requires. But in addition, you must keep a set of books using the LERN Financial Format, or you will not be able to manage your finances and your program will be in jeopardy.

How the Financial Format Works

Here are the unique aspects of the Financial Format:

1. **Promotion is separated from Production expenses.** This is critical for you as a manager to understand whether or not your promotion is working, whether promotion is the problem, or whether it is the solution.

2. **Percentages are stated.** More important than dollars in your financial analysis are the percentages. By getting your percentages in line, you can get your dollars in line.

3. **Operating Margin.** This is not an expense, but what is left

over after you take your direct costs from your income. This is where the game is being played right now. If you can get a good Operating Margin, then you can improve your financial performance. If you cannot, then there is no way you can improve your financial performance.

Use this Format for your total program, for each division, and for each class or activity.

Program. This is your total unit or organization, however you define it. It should be a unit totally devoted to offering lifelong learning programs, however, because you do not want to mix your finances for lifelong learning programming with other types of services or activities.

Division. This is a unit or subdivision within your overall Program. We recommend you have between five and ten Divisions within your overall Program.

A Division can be based on any one of the following:

Type of subject matter, for example computers, arts and crafts, nursing, engineering, recreation, science, and so on.

Audience, for example children, teens, older adults, nurses, engineers, executives, secretaries, and so on.

Format, for example trips and tours, one night seminars, weekend programs, and so on.

What you will find is that your Divisions function as different animals and behave in different ways financially. They have different financial patterns. So you want to analyze each Division separately.

Class or Event. These are individual activities that make up a Division.

Ideal Percentages

So then the question is "What are the ideal percentages for a successful lifelong learning program?"

The following are ideal percentages for an average program or cumulative averages for a variety of different kinds of programming. In other LERN publications, we detail different ideal percentages for various or specific types of programming. But before understanding what those percentages are for your type of programming, it is necessary to know the ideal percentages for an average program overall.

Here is the answer:

Income. Income is always 100%.

Promotion. Promotion should be in the 10%-15% range overall for your total program.

Production. Production should be 45%-50% of your income.

Total Direct Costs. This figure should be 60%. These numbers come from successful programs, from ten years of research by LERN, and from the more recent work of Philip Whatley, who has enhanced our knowledge of finances. Whatley says that the information sector and indeed service sector as a whole has 60% Direct Costs and 40% Operating Margin.

Operating Margin. This figure is 40%. If it is more than 40%, you are doing well. If it is less than 40%, you will find it very difficult to become financially self-sufficient.

Administration Costs. Since what falls into administration costs varies so much by institution, this is an arbitrary number reached by subtracting surplus or net from the Operating Margin.

Net. Surplus or net is put at a modest 5%, achievable but not overly ambitious.

What Constitutes Financial Self-Sufficiency

With that background, we can now address the question of what constitutes financial sufficiency for program.

Programs can be financially self-sufficient. New programs, however, are exempted from financial self-sufficiency. New programs, like any new business or venture, cannot make money on the first day. As with every other start-up, there is an initial period of investment and losing money until it breaks even and then begins to make money. If your program is less than two years old, it should not be expected to be financially self-sufficient — yet.

Programs more than two years old can be financially self-sufficient. Financial self-sufficiency benefits at least three constituencies:

1. It benefits the institution because the program is then a net

plus, or contributor to the overall institution's financial stability, not a negative or drain on the institution's resources.

2. It benefits the program's executive and staff, because they are paying or covering their own salaries and thus their positions and unit's existence are secure.

3. It benefits the public, the state and society, those who benefit from the program. These people, companies and organizations receive valuable services and education critical to a healthy economy and maintaining an educated citizenry.

So what, for a lifelong learning operation, is financial self-sufficiency?

In the for-profit sector it means covering all your costs. After that, you start making a profit.

In the non-profit sector, institutions are not expected to generate fee income to cover all their costs. They are supplemented by grants, donations, tax support and so on. Within a non-profit institution, financial self-sufficiency for a program means covering all of its own costs.

Thus, a program that covers its Direct Costs and Program Administration is financially self-sufficient.

In our chart of nine boxes on the next page, a program in box 5 is financially self-sufficient. A program in boxes 6, 7, 8 or 9 is making money. A program in boxes 1, 2, 3 or 4 is losing money.

Any program that is in boxes 5-9 should not be eliminated, because it is financially not costing the institution anything. Any unit in boxes 1-4 is costing the institution financially, and needs to be improved financially to achieve financial self-sufficiency.

Institutional Overhead

Institutional Overhead cost, no matter how it is calculated, is part of the Net. Whether Institutional Overhead is charged as a percentage of income, a percentage of expenses, or a flat figure, it is still financially recorded as part of the Net.

If Institutional Overhead or costs are recorded as an expense to the program, the program may very well appear to be losing money.

This is damaging in at least two ways:

Financial Format

Income	$____ ____%
Promotion	$____ ____%
Production	$____ ____%
Direct Costs	$____ ____%
Operating Margin	$____ ____%
Administration	$____ ____%
Net	$____ ____%

1. If the program appears to be losing money, wrong conclusions and actions could ensue. If the program is actually financially self-sufficient and making money, then it would be detrimental indeed to judge it losing money.
2. The perception of losing money, especially if it is false, is certainly a negative motivation to the staff and the unit. Inaccurate record keeping will not be a positive reinforcement of the staff and its efforts. That motivation and effort, of course, is key to improving financial performance.

After your program has achieved financial self-sufficiency, it is reasonable to expect the unit to contribute financially to the institution. The most common way this is done is by assigning it a portion of Institutional Overhead or costs.

You can budget a Net profit or surplus objective for your program, and that Net surplus can go to cover Institutional Overhead (or any other expenses you deem important).

Thus, the way to apportion Institutional Overhead is to budget it as expected Net surplus or profit. If the unit does not meet budget, that is one thing. But to say that the program is "losing money" because it has not covered all of the Institutional Overhead expected of it, is not correct and very misleading for all concerned. It is not in the best interests of your institution to perceive your program as "losing money" when it is really making money.

Costs Paid by the Institution

If there are program costs paid for by the institution, they should be allocated to Direct Costs or Program Administration for a true reading of the program's financial performance.

While this is occurring less frequently, some managers report to us that their institutions pick up some costs of the program. Examples of these costs are brochure printing, benefits for instructors, postage, and some staff positions, such as the executive.

Just as it is troublesome to report your unit "losing money" when it is actually financially self-sufficient, it is equally troublesome to report your unit is "making money" when the institution is covering any Direct Costs or Program Administration expenses.

Ideal Percentages

Income	$_____	<u>100</u> %
Promotion	$_____	<u>10-15</u> %
Production	$_____	<u>45-50</u>%
Direct Costs	$_____	<u>60</u> %
Operating Margin	$_____	<u>40</u> %
Administration	$_____	<u>35</u> %
Net	$____	<u>5</u> %

Setting Up Budgets

In devising your budget for the coming year, you need to do the opposite of what comes naturally.

What comes naturally is to outline all your projected expenses for the year, including all the salaries you want to pay and the computers you want to buy, and then figure out how much income you must generate to make money.

The problem here is two-fold. First, you always have more expenses than you can afford. And second, this approach leads to income stretching, trying to justify more income than you can reasonably expect.

If we all took this approach in real life, we would decide how much it costs to live for a year, and then go to the boss and tell her or him what salary we need for the year. Obviously, it doesn't work that way. And it doesn't work that way for your program either.

Instead, you start with your income. You figure out what income you will have for the year, and then you fit your expenses within the income projected. After you have figured out a dollar figure for your total income, you want to express it as a percentage. Your total income is 100%.

After you calculate your income, you next figure out your surplus. Surplus is what's left over after all your expenses. Surplus has a variety of purposes. The first is to make sure you don't lose any money — a sort of safety net. As you know, just projecting income doesn't give you that amount, and a surplus allows a little leeway.

A second purpose of surplus is to generate funds for expansion and program development. With the extra money generated you can add a new staff person, develop a new program, or upgrade computers. A third purpose of surplus is to make the central institution happy and thus ensure your program's continuation and your job. By being an income and surplus generator, rather than a cost center or money drainer, your program and job will both have enhanced stability.

Even if all your surplus goes back to the institution at the end of the year, your surplus gives you bargaining power for the things you want for your program.

An ideal surplus for your program is 7%. An acceptable surplus is 4%. More than 7% means you are doing very well for your institution. Between 4% and 7% means you are definitely both financially self-sufficient and contributing to the institution. Between 0% surplus and 4% surplus means you are financially self-sufficient, but just a little improvement in the numbers would help solidify your position.

Before you claim a surplus of 10% or 20% for your program, review our definition of surplus to include your General & Administrative expenses.

That is the real crunch these days, the real challenge. Generating money over your direct costs is good and necessary, but in order for you to be truly standing on your own two feet, and for your central administration to know that, you need also cover your G&A expenses.

Here's what we have so far:

Income $_____   100%
Surplus $_____   xx%
Total left so far: 100 - xx% = _____

Example. We want a surplus of 4%. xx% = 4%. We now have 96% of income left for expenses.

Next we figure refunds. Refunds are income given back after you have cancelled classes. Refunds might include income returned because of dissatisfaction with the class or extenuating circumstances for your participants. Refunds do NOT include cancelled class income, which should not show up as income in the first place.

Your refund rate should definitely be less than 4%. If it is more than that, you may have some problems with quality in your programs. Or you may have a refund policy that is too liberal. Before reaching that conclusion, however, examine the reasons for the refunds and whether you have good program quality.

Example. Last year's refund rate was 2%. So we budget the same percentage this year.

Promotion costs come next. As promotion is really an investment, and you won't be able to generate your income without your promotion investment, you don't want to cut your promotional dollars. Instead, you want to maximize your investment. You want your promotional dollars to work harder for you.

Review your last year's financial statement. That percentage is one place to start. From there you can go on to play some 'what if' games. Are there any examples of where you spent more on promotion than your overall average? If so, what was your experience? Did that activity generate more income, or less? Did some kinds of promotional efforts, such as direct mail, do better than other kinds, such as advertising? Can you redirect some monies into other kinds of promotional efforts to maximize the money?

If you are going to budget promotion as less of a percentage of income this year than you did last year, you will need to justify that. There will need to be a good reason why promotional costs are less. In general, if it costs your program $1 to generate $5, that ratio will hold true within a wide range of dollars. If you cut back on promotion, you are also cutting back on income. And the other way around — if you increase promotion costs, you should be able to increase your income. Where this does not hold true is if you increase promotional expenditures but put the extra investment into wasted efforts, or if you cut back on promotion and the cutbacks are on wasted efforts. But without clear evidence of "wasted efforts," an increase or decrease in promotional expenditures will lead to a proportional increase or decrease in income.

That is why it is so critical to set promotional expenditures next, and to be very, very careful before you cut them. Your promotional expenditures are an investment that has a direct relation to your income.

Next set your production expenses. Again, look at last year's expenses for production and use that percentage as a guide for this year.

If your production expenses are going to be different from what they were last year, there has to be a reason.

Setting your promotion and production expenses using percentage figures from last year, or the previous two to three years experience is not your final figure for these expenses, but it is the place to start.

After you have reviewed the overall budget figures, making them add up to 100%, then you can go into much more detail, looking at the production and promotion expenses and seeing if your figures add up.

It is important in building your annual budget to build initially from the top down. That is, come up with some overall figures first. Then you can build from the bottom up, calculating line items for each expense.

Now let's see where we are in our example:

Income   100%
Surplus   4%
Refunds   2%
Promotion   15%
Production   40%

What's left is 39%. This is what we can allocate to General & Administrative expenses, our G&A.

Chapter 7
Marketing

Core Marketing Concepts

Everything We Do is Marketing

As every practitioner knows, the world is divided into two parts: "us" and "them." Until recently, we have always started thinking about marketing with "us." What is our organization, what is our mission, what does our boss want, what is our institutional charter, what are our activities and services (our products), and most importantly, how can we get "them" to buy products from "us?"

Normally, when we think of marketing we think of getting out the brochures. If the printer has had a good day and doesn't print our brochure upside down, and if the postmaster has had an even better day and expedites our mailing, then we heave a huge sigh of relief and say we have done a good job of marketing.

But there is something more important than what we send out to "them," and that is what they send back to "us."

Our participants send back to us more than registrations, more than money. They send back to us an image — an image of what they think about our organization, our products, our people.

Thus, the place to start thinking about marketing is not with "us" but with "them." That is why more and more successful practitioners are looking at the demographics of their audiences, surveying participants, doing more extensive evaluations, and developing a better customer relations program. Today, we need to start with our participants when developing or improving our marketing.

If our participants send an image back to us, then we too send more than just brochures out to our audiences. Thus, marketing is not simply sending brochures out. We will discuss that later in depth as part of "promotion," which is a subset of marketing. But more than brochures, marketing is everything we do to portray our organization to our audiences.

Every point of contact with our audiences, and thus almost everything we do, is marketing.

Some of the ways we portray our organization include:

- The place where we hold our programs
- Our price
- Our stationery
- The way we reject potential teachers
- How we say "hello"
- Our hold button — how long is someone on hold, is there music, what kind of music?
- Our course/event selection
- Our phone number

We Want to Segment the Market

There is no such thing as "the general public," says Philip Kotler, the father of marketing for nonprofits. There are only "general publics."

The concept of breaking down one's audience into many audiences, or segments, began first in industry. William Draves, LERN President, notes, "When I was growing up and went to my grandfather's house for the weekend, he had three breakfast cereals available in the morning. One was puffed rice (yeach), one was corn flakes, and the "new kid" on the block was probably Wheaties. Now there are a zillion cereals, fruit this and chocolate that.

"The cereal that has probably segmented the market the most is Grape-Nuts. Some time ago, Grape-Nuts ran a commercial with a guy on horseback riding up to the top of the Rocky Mountains. The guy gets off the horse and opens up his saddle bag, and, of course, takes out a half gallon of milk, and pours it on his cereal. Now there is only a sliver of the American population that thinks riding on a horse is fun, and only a few people who get their kicks out of climbing to the top of the Rockies (there's no air up there), so the number of people who BOTH like horses and high altitudes is only a half-percent, say, of the cereal-eating population. No matter, those are the people Grape-Nuts is after. They don't care about those who want sugar, chocolate, flakes or anything else. They are going after a narrow segment of the market."

The concept of market segmentation has recently spread to the non-profit and service sector as well. We have never really served everyone; we have always served some but not all demographic or social groups. Within those populations we DO serve, it is ever more critical to be aware of the differences among our market segments. Before now, we have tended to lump those we serve into one "average."

But today we want to move away from lumping our participants together and seeing what they have in common. Instead, we want to differentiate our participants and find out what makes each significant group different from others. That process is called market segmentation.

What market segmentation allows us to do is to serve each group better, and thus gain more enrollments from each of our market segments. The sum total then is more overall enrollments. By lumping our participants together and trying to avoid distinctions, we gear our programs and promotions to some mythical "average" person who doesn't really exist, and consequently miss many of our potential participants. The way to strengthen our programs and improve our enrollments is to segment our markets. The primary way organizations differentiate their customers is by demographic variables. The most commonly used demographic variables in market segmentation for continuing professional education, seminars and conferences are:

- SIC code (Standard Industrial Classification code)
- Company size
- Job title
- Geography

53

The most commonly used demographic variables in market segmentation for community courses and events are:
- Geography
- Sex
- Age
- Education level

One need not use all of the demographic variables. That would be unnecessary, time consuming and in the end probably self-defeating due to the volume of data. Instead, pick out one, then two, and then maybe three demographic variables that are most important in distinguishing the market segments for your program.

The biggest advantage of market segmentation is in the way you as an administrator think about your participants and your potential audience. When you start to think in terms of market segmentation, a new approach to marketing evolves.

We Are Part of the Direct Marketing Business

Direct marketing differs from advertising in general because it can be measured, and we can find out what works and what doesn't work. General advertising, on the other hand, can't be measured. They say that half of all advertising is wasted, we just don't know what half.

An illustration: Several years ago the state of Alaska put an advertisement on the Super Bowl telling people to come to Alaska the next summer. Before they put the expensive ad on television, they had no idea of how well it would do. After the ad ran, they had no idea of how well the ad did. And even after the summer tourism season, when more people did in fact come to Alaska than before, they had no idea of how well the ad did.

The increase could have come from the Super Bowl ad. But it also could have been because travelers were wary of international travel that summer due to overseas discontent. Or it could have been because Alaskan mosquitoes were at an all-time low that summer. The Alaskan advertisers still have no idea if the ad contributed to the increase in tourism.

In contrast, you can determine how effective your brochure is. You can determine how effective each type of distribution of your brochure is. You can determine how effective a second mailing of your brochure would be. You can determine if mailing to every household works, or whether an expensive rented mailing list works better.

Programming is part of the direct marketing business. It is sometimes called the direct mail business. It is sometimes called the "junk mail" business. But because direct mail is being increasingly targeted to those people who want the service and away from those who are not interested, the term "junk mail" may become an obsolete one. Today, a major marketing theme is to send one's brochures only to those most likely to become participants, and thus to those most interested in receiving it.

Getting your brochure into the hands of someone interested in your program is direct marketing.

Here are the major characteristics of direct marketing:

a. There is a measurable response. Unlike an ad on television, the response to direct marketing can be measured.

b. We can track the success of different kinds of promotion. Not only can the overall success be measured, but we can find out what kinds of promotion work better than others. We can find out whether distributing brochures in public libraries is successful; whether mailing to the Chamber of Commerce list of businesses works; whether inserting the brochure in a newspaper works.

c. We can test various aspects of our promotion. We don't have to take big gambles on a new promotional idea. Instead, we can test new brochure distribution ideas and find out if they work before distributing large numbers of brochures and dropping another kind of brochure distribution.

d. There are mathematical relationships in promotion.

Some illustrations:

• If our test is successful, for example, then it is most likely that a broader distribution will be successful as well.

- If we cut our brochure distribution in half without any prior analysis, we know we will likely cut our enrollments in half as well.
- We can measure promotion as a percentage of income, the cost to obtain a new participant, the cost to retain an existing participant, and much more.

Key Statistics in Direct Marketing of Programs

Response Rate — This is how many brochures it takes to get one registration, on average.

To find this figure, divide the number of registrations for one session by the number of brochures distributed for that session. Secondly, determine your response rate over the course of a year. Take the number of registrations for one year and divide by brochures distributed for the year. The more sophisticated programs then find out if there are seasonal variations in the response rate. For example, maybe it takes more brochures in winter to get one registration than it does in the fall or spring. Knowing the seasonal or session variations from your overall average helps to improve your distribution even more.

A registration is one person registering for one class/event. One person registering for two classes/events is two registrations.

For example, if we distribute 50,000 brochures and get 2,000 registrations, our response rate is 4.0 percent.

Average Participants Per Class/Event — This is the average number of persons to be found in a class/event in your program.

To find this figure, divide the total number of registrations for a year by the total number of classes run. DO NOT include the canceled classes/events in your total of "classes offered."

Direct marketing ratios and concepts hold the keys to being able to market successfully today. We can measure our success and thereby improve upon it.

We Should Market Affectively, Not Just Cognitively

The "affective" realm is the heart, the guts, the feelings of a person. The "cognitive" realm is the brain and what we know.

Lifelong learning programming has traditionally seen its job as to funnel information and facts to people; to relay information from a teacher to the students. But that fundamental nature of our business is changing. Facts and information can be readily obtained from a computer these days, and our classes are evolving more into human communication involving much more than facts and information, and instead involving our interpretation, application, meaning, relevance and relationships.

We have also traditionally believed people have come to our programs for "skills and knowledge." We now know this is only partially true. People also come to our programs to meet other people, to enhance their self-esteem, to enjoy themselves, and for a host of other legitimate, important reasons that involve, but are not limited by "skills and knowledge."

The marketing implication of these shifts is that we should market affectively, not just cognitively. We want to create a feeling about our program through our promotion. We want to look to market to people's emotions and feelings, not just to their heads.

In *Positioning: The Battle for Your Mind*, authors Ries and Trout note that a person has a one-quart container sitting on his shoulders, and that the brain can hold only so much information.

Your program and every other organization and product out there are competing for a place in that limited amount of brain space. To position your program in your participants' minds, Ries and Trout say, you need to establish a position that is easily remembered.

Throwing out facts and figures and information and rationales is not easily remembered. Some things that help establish a position in participants' minds include:

- Your program's name. A short name can be remembered, a long one cannot.
- A slogan. A good slogan will create a niche in your participants' minds and help them remember your program.

- A logo. A logo is a visual slogan. It identifies your program visually. It is effective for creating that position in a person's mind.

Your brochure cover is a primary medium to market affectively. The graphic design or picture should create an emotion or feeling that exemplifies your program.

Your course descriptions should be written in "you" language, stressing benefits, outcomes and end results. Your course descriptions can be written to impact a person affectively and emotionally, not just cognitively.

By marketing affectively, we often reach our participants with a message that is more effective, and more important than mere facts, figures, information, skills and knowledge. The long-term impact of your course or program may be that which reaches the feelings, emotions, guts and hearts of your participants.

In today's competitive marketing environment, four new concepts help define our marketing approach and strategy. To repeat, they are:

1. Everything we do is marketing.
2. We want to segment the market.
3. We are part of the direct marketing business.
4. We want to market affectively, not just cognitively.

To return to our diagram of "Us" and "Them," we must acknowledge that the world has changed and it is no longer us versus them. It is us serving them. Marketing, then, is not glitz, hype or a sales con job. Marketing is a two-way communication flow. In successful marketing, your listening to your participants is more important than your talking to your participants.

Because marketing is two-way communication, marketing does not promise, it delivers. It is not separate from the quality of your programs. It is integral to the quality of your programs. The worst thing you can have is to have a successful promotional effort and lousy quality. Because then people won't come back, and you won't have much of a program. Good marketing enhances the quality of your program. It may challenge your staff and instructors to achieve greater quality, and it may demand that your program deliver what it promises. But that too is in the best interests of your participants. And what is in the best interests of your participants is in your program's best interests as well.

Marketing is not something that a specialist in your organization "does." It is a way of thinking, an approach that everyone in your organization is involved in, and it is the linking of your participants with the quality of your programs.

Developing a One-Year Marketing Plan

There is no substitute for having a written marketing plan. A one-year marketing plan is a specific promotional plan for generating the registrations needed to make budget.

Here are the elements that should go into a one-year marketing plan:

1. Enrollment objectives, by session
2. Number of classes, by session, and by division, needed to meet enrollment objectives
3. Number of brochures needed to generate enrollment objectives, by session
4. Brochure distribution plan — number of brochures for each kind of distribution (in-house mailing list; rented lists; libraries; fairs, etc.) — along with the expected return response for each kind of brochure distribution. For example, you might expect a 10 percent return rate from your in-house list and a half-percent return rate from a rented list.
5. Dates of execution for each kind of brochure distribution
6. Person assigned responsibility for each kind of brochure distribution
7. Other promotional activities, including publicity, advertising, open houses, press releases etc.
8. Timetable, a week-by-week schedule of promotional activities to be conducted for the entire year

Without a written marketing plan, it is unlikely a program can successfully execute the plan and improve its success. With a written annual plan, the only thing left to do is to execute.

The Three Most Essential Marketing Practices

There are three essential marketing practices to do in order for your program to succeed. This is true whether you are with a small organization or a large one, whether you are in charge of marketing or it is just one of your functions.

1. Think marketing. We really cannot succeed in marketing our program without thinking about marketing. This does not always come naturally, as many programmers come from a content, teaching or liberal arts background.

Marketing knowledge, therefore, must be acquired on the job. Read at least one marketing book a year. Read marketing columns in magazines and newsletters. Then think about marketing, about your participants, their needs, and how to communicate with them.

Thinking about marketing does not have to be done every day, but if it is not done regularly, you are not likely to be successful.

2. Have a written plan. The "plan" can be written on the back of an envelope. Some of the best marketing plans are written on cocktail napkins.

The key point is that it is "written." If you have it in your head, you don't really have it. It doesn't have to be written in complete sentences; it doesn't have to be more than one page long; but it does have to be in writing.

Without a written plan, we have no way to achieve our marketing objectives.

3. Execute. Whatever is written down, do. Your written plan is your ticket to marketing success. Executing the plan fulfills that success.

Execution is grunt and grind work. It is labeling another thousand brochures, licking another 10 stamps, driving another 10 miles. But when the plan is executed, success can result.

If execution is only half-done, your program will fall short of its objectives. If you do it, they will come. If you don't do it, don't expect them to come.

Think, Have, Execute — Marketing. T-H-E-M. And that's what marketing is all about: serving "them," your participants.

Chapter 8
Promotion

Effective Promotion

Promotion is a subset of marketing. While everything you do that has a point of contact with your audience is marketing, not everything you do is promotion. Promotion is an activity which leads to a direct result in registrations and income.

There are four major kinds of promotion, based on these criteria:

- **How it reaches people**
  - **Individual.** The promotion reaches people on an individual basis, like a letter or brochure.
  - **Mass.** The promotion reaches people all together, like a television commercial.
- **Cost**
  - **Paid.** The promotion has a direct cost, such as an advertisement.
  - **Unpaid.** The promotion has no direct cost, even though there may be time and effort involved, such as a public service announcement.

	Individual	Mass
Paid	*Direct Marketing*	*Advertising*
Unpaid	*Customer Service*	*eMarketing*

If a promotion reaches people on an individual basis and we pay for it, we call that **direct marketing**. This is your brochure and its distribution.

If a promotion reaches people on a mass basis and we pay for it, we call that **advertising**. This is an advertisement in the newspaper or on radio.

If a promotion reaches people on a mass basis and is unpaid, we call that **publicity**. A public service announcement on radio or a newspaper story are examples of publicity. E-mail and website marketing are now major venues for publicity.

If a promotion reaches people on an individual basis and is unpaid, we call that **customer service**. Talking on the phone with a potential participant is one example. Following up by calling or answering recent inquiries by e-mail is another example.

The question is always asked where to put one's time, money and resources. Should we have a booth at the county fair? Should we pass out balloons with our name on them on street corners? Should we be speaking before civic clubs?

Different businesses in different industries rely on different mixes of the above for maximum effectiveness. In our business, for our field, the best use of time, effort and money for promotion breaks down roughly like this:

- 75% Direct Marketing: Brochure and brochure distribution. Put about three-quarters of your promotional effort into your brochure and brochure distribution. It is by far the single most critical element in your promotion.
- 10%-15% E-marketing and Publicity: E-mail, your web site, newspaper stories and public service announcements (PSAs). E-marketing is now the second most important promotion method for most programs, next only to brochures.
- 5%-10% Advertising: Newspaper, radio or cable TV ads. Advertising is no replacement for your brochure and brochure distribution, but it can be a part of your promotional mix to supplement the brochure effort. The more sophisticated programs do have advertising campaigns to supplement brochure distribution. Advertising on the web would also fall into this category.

- 5% Customer Service. Phone calls and e-mail. Spend two days a year training your staff in customer relations. This is one of the most productive uses of staff time — training and relating to customers — and will yield results. It doesn't take much time or cost much money, but it has a big impact.

10 Most Important Promotion Things to Do

Every year marketing expert Paul Franklin of Portland, OR, sits down with William Draves to come up with the Top 10 new promotional techniques of the year. Recently the two also came up with the 10 Most Important Marketing Things to Do. While the list is specific to seminars, conferences and continuing professional education, it may be relevant for other kinds of programming as well.

1. Know your 7 primary segments.

Only seven segments of your mailing list give you 80 percent of your income. You need to know your seven primary audiences by demographic segmentation. Design programs for them, promote to them. Your marketing efforts should concentrate on your top seven segments. For non-participants, the most likely people to attend are those in your seven primary demographic segments.

2. Mail early.

Whatever you do, get the brochure out on time. And the earlier the better (translation: more registrations). Try mailing two weeks earlier for your next event, and see the impact. Don't hold up your brochure for last-minute program changes, design changes, or your third proofreading. Get the brochure in the mail, early.

3. Have a one-year marketing plan.

Begin your planning one year ahead of time. Develop your plan and stick to the timeline. The marketing plan does not have to be long, but it must be in writing. Include objectives, and what you will do to meet those objectives. Include deadlines, and who is responsible for each activity.

4. Mail three times to your best people.

Your best people are past participants and people from your seven primary segments who live close to where the event is being held. Past participants are your most important best people. If you can, mail the third brochure in an envelope with a letter. Or send a post card. But hit them up three times.

5. Have cutting-edge content.

Good promotion can't sell an event that doesn't have cutting-edge program content. Some 20 percent or more of the event content should be new every year. Developing cutting-edge content that appeals to your seven primary audiences is essential to marketing success.

6. Survey past participants.

Survey past participants for things like: what month, week or days to hold the event; what time of year is best; what city is best; what seminar topics you should offer; what hotel is most preferred. Survey past participants, not non-participants.

7. Do last-month promotion.

Last-month promotion can be broadcast faxes, e-mail and post cards. Telephone calls take time but are effective. Do not mail brochures in the last month, except to people in the local area. Last-month promotion is following up and repeating marketing to those most likely to attend.

8. Do an e-mail newsletter.

Past participants should receive a regular e-mail newsletter with tips and ideas and things they want to read. Included in the regular e-mail newsletter are notices and promotional copy for your up-coming events and programs.

9. Web site for major events.

For every major event, have one or more web site pages with complete information. Add color and small graphics to keep it lively. Be sure to include online registration. The more information you can provide on your web site, the better.

10. Analyze registration data.

Analyze the registration data from your last event to determine what lists to rent and audiences to target based on your seven primary segments. As soon as your event is over, critique it. Make improvements to your marketing plan for the next event.

Chapter 9
Brochures

Designing the Brochure with AIDA

When thinking about designing your continuing education brochure, it is very helpful to think in terms of the AIDA principle. This gives you a systematic way to organize your thinking and energy in getting your brochure to be as effective as possible.

The AIDA principle was developed for promotional materials to respond to the way people read and react to promotions. Marketing experts tell us that three seconds is about all you have to capture someone's attention before they make a decision, usually unconsciously, whether to continue reading or stop and look at something else. If someone continues reading, that person will generally spend only another 30 seconds before making another, again usually unconscious, decision whether to continue reading or stop. Finally, if someone continues reading that person will, on average, give your brochure 3 minutes of attention. Marketers call this the 3-30-3 rule. The AIDA principle was developed to maximize your brochure's effectiveness in responding to the 3-30-3 rule.

In the continuing education field, the formula and format for success differ somewhat between those brochures for community classes, and those brochures promoting continuing professional education.

A = Attention
The first A in the AIDA principle stands for "Attention."

The function of the front cover of your brochure is to attract the attention of your prospective participants and to motivate readers to pick up your brochure, open it, and begin reading.

Thus the most effective continuing education covers are designed to get someone's attention within 3 seconds, and to stimulate the reader to give the brochure more than 3 seconds of time by opening it and beginning to read.

For continuing professional education brochures, the cover often contains a visual image, such as a picture, that generates an emotional response promoting such ideals as success, respect, career advancement, and results. For some work-related brochures, usually for specific events, an event title, color and/or visual design can replace the visual image, provided the cover evokes some kind of positive emotional response and thus stimulates the reader to read on.

For community class brochures, a large visual image, usually a photograph, is an essential part of the formula for a successful brochure cover.

For all brochure covers, the general rule for success is to keep the number of words on the cover to a minimum. The focus of the brochure cover should be on a need or want of your audience. Your organization's name appears on the cover, but with lower visibility, understanding that your audience responds to your program's content more than your name.

I = Interest

Once a reader decides to give your brochure more than 3 seconds of time, the next challenge is to interest the reader in your program. You have roughly 30 seconds to interest your readers, and you do that on pages 2 and 3 of the brochure.

For continuing professional education brochures, there are generally two best messages to convey on pages 2 and 3. The first is that your program meets the reader's needs in terms of outcomes and results. This is accomplished by creating paragraphs focusing on the reader's interest in outcomes, benefits, results, and why the person should attend. The other best message to convey on pages 2 and 3 is why the person should attend your program and not another program. This is often done with a paragraph or copy on why your organization is unique, what distinct or exclusive benefits or information will be covered, or why your instructors are experts or authorities.

For community program brochures, there are two best messages to convey on pages 2 and 3. The first is that your program has an interesting array or diversity of offerings. That array or diversity of offerings is shown by listing the categories of courses in your Table of Contents. The best use of page 3 for community program brochures is for the Table of Contents. At the same time, the Table of Contents is organized by category of courses so that the reader can find one or more areas of interest quickly and be able to get to the pages of greatest interest quickly. The other best message to convey on pages 2 and 3 for community program brochures is your program's uniqueness. You want to state why someone should attend your program, identify your organization's best strengths from your participants' perspective, and convey a warm and welcoming atmosphere for prospective participants.

D = Desire

Once a reader decides to give your brochure more than 30 seconds of attention and interest, you want the reader to move quickly to the content of your program and create a desire on the part of the reader to register and participate. Using the 3-30-3 rule, you have about 3 minutes to create that desire and invite the person to register.

For community program brochures, your course descriptions create that desire. The course titles are most important and should be boldfaced in black ink in order to stand out prominently. The title is followed by a 40 – 120 word description of the outcomes, results and benefits of the course. After the description, the logistics of instructor, time, place and fee are listed. At various points throughout the brochure, it is also good practice to point out the page number of your registration information, and/or provide some of the ways and numbers in which a person can register, such as online and the URL, or by phone and the phone number.

For continuing professional education brochures with a number of courses or offerings, the formula for success is the same as for community program brochures. That is, course descriptions with title, description and logistics create that desire. For professional continuing education brochures for single courses, or events such as seminars and conferences, the formula differs somewhat. In the case of single courses and events, the description of the event takes up as much space as you need for it to be effective, and usually includes a more detailed outline of the agenda as well as more copy about the instructor/s qualifications and expertise.

A = Action

The second or final A in AIDA stands for Action. Action is registering with your program.

For all brochures, registration information and registration form should be at or near the end of the brochure. On pages 2 and/or 3, you can list the page where a reader can find the registration information and form, but you should not give any registration details on the first few pages of the brochure.

For all brochures, a registration form should be included. Even though more people are registering online, and even though your organization should encourage people to register online, you still want to have a registration form in the brochure. The form itself is a marketing message that tells the read to take action.

For all brochures, readers should have as many different ways to register as possible. Online registration should be offered. You can encourage people to register online. But individuals have different preferred ways of purchasing. Thus, your organization will get more registrations if you provide as many other ways of registering as possible. For most programs, that means including by phone and by mail. Offer other options of registering if they apply to your audience, such as walk-in registration at your office and registering via fax or e-mail or text messaging. Successful programs almost always have at least 4 ways to register.

For almost every continuing education program, the brochure generates the majority of registrations for the program. At the time of this writing direct marketers in other industries are mailing more catalogs even as more people purchase online. In the continuing education field, the brochure, along with e-mail promotion, is essential. Some programs have found out the hard way by temporarily dropping the brochure, and suffered significant drops in registrations. If there is a time when programs can or should drop the brochure without hurting registrations significantly, LERN will let you know. Spend the majority of your promotion resources on your brochures, because in the continuing education field a good brochure one of the essentials.

Chapter 10
eMarketing

Mastering Your Web Site: AIDA Still Applies

Your web site or home page on the Internet is becoming an increasingly popular and important marketing tool. All evidence is that promoting your program through your web site on the Internet will grow in effectiveness. And there is tremendous potential for your web site to register participants and reduce registration staff time enormously. So there are many good reasons why developing a good home page or web site is important.

In reviewing a number of LERN members' web sites, there is one overwhelming conclusion: AIDA still applies. AIDA is the formula for a good brochure —

A = Attract
I = Interest
D = Desire
A = Action

and it is clear that those four words apply to the Internet just as much as to your brochure.

ATTRACT

Access to your program has to be visible from the first page the viewer sees on the Internet. Most programs are parts of a larger institution, and thus part of that institution's home page or web site. In order for people to find you easily and quickly, you need to have your name and access to your program from the main menu or first page of your institution's web site.

The first page viewers see should be attractive, with color and good graphics, making people want to continue.

INTEREST

On your program's first page, put your unique selling proposition (USP) and a paragraph about what your program is and why someone would want to participate. Many web sites we visited simply went from their name to their classes, forgetting to tell people who they are and why someone should be interested. Make sure you tell folks right up front why they should keep looking at your program.

On your program's first page, you want the Internet equivalent of a Table of Contents. Make sure the choices are clear and understandable to your readers.

DESIRE

Run a description of your courses. Don't just list titles. Have the full description for each of your activities listed and available for viewing.

ACTION

Include registration as one of the options a person can move to from your program's first page. Always look to move people to registration.

Eight Marketing Strategies that Work

Some strategies for marketing on the Internet work. Others do not work. Here are the top eight strategies that currently are the most successful.

1. Brochure-web mix

Your brochure and web site should play off each other. On your home page, have a picture of your latest brochure cover. In your brochure, keep telling people your web site URL. On your web site, have a place where people can sign up to be on your mailing list to get your brochure. In your brochure, stress registering online.

2. Email promotions

Email promotions are popular, and they work. As people can unsubscribe at any time, your e-mails are never spam. Email promotions have joined the brochure as an essential promotion strategy for just about every offering of classes and events.

3. Get links to your site

Encourage other organizations and companies to have a link to your web site. Look for organizations that do not compete with you, but offer a complementary or different service or information. Look for one-way links, and try to avoid reciprocating since you don't want people to leave your site.

4. Catchy domain names

Catchy domain names that your audience can remember are a powerful marketing tool. Avoid using your organization's initials as your domain name, or your institution's URL with a slash (/) after it for your program. People can't remember initials or long URLs. Instead, find a catchy and unused phrase like *www. ChicagoTraining.org* or *www.WorldClassEducation.org*.

5. Search engine listings

Get a high listing on search engines is an important marketing strategy. Instead of trying to compete for a high listing for a broad keyword search term like "continuing education" or "training," try for a high listing for a much more narrow keyword search where there are fewer competitors.

6. E-mail autoresponders

In your brochure, newspaper ads, flyers and publicity, give people a special e-mail address to write to, such as *courses@*. Then create a "vacation message" that gives people information about your program, plus links to your web site and online registration. This gives people immediate feedback and you get their e-mail address for follow-up.

7. Online registration

Online registration works. Get secure server software or contract with a company that has the software on their server. Take credit cards. Avoid telling people to print the page and mail or fax it in. Instead, have them register for classes online and pay for it with credit cards. This is the way of the future.

8. Web descriptions that sell

Create web descriptions that sell your courses. Design your web site so people can find any course in three clicks. Show categories of events or courses off your home page. And have a link to online registration at the end of every course or event description. For more specifics and how-to step-by-step procedures, see LERN's manual "Successful Web Sites."

Ten Do's and Don'ts
for Successful Email Promotions

Email promotions should now be included as part of your promotion mix. They are effective with most audiences. From an analysis of successful e-mail promotions, here are seven do's and don'ts on successful e-mail promotions.

1. Keep it short

Email promotions should be short, no more than 10 paragraphs long, with four paragraphs being an ideal length. Paragraphs should be one to four sentences long, not more.

2. Offer info options

Offer as many ways as possible to get more information or have questions answered. Options include phone number, e-mail

address (a person works better than "info"), getting flyer or brochure faxed, PDF brochure online, and if available, a brochure
snail mailed to them.

3. Link to web site

Provide a link to your web site for more information and registration.

The link should be to the exact page in your web site concern-
ing the event. Do not link merely to your program's Home Page.
Don't make someone search for the web description.

The e-mail promotion should have wording such as, "For complete information, click here at *http://www.xxxx*" or "Click below
and you will be taken directly to..."

4. Unsubscribe

Always include an "unsubscribe" option. The unsubscribe option gives your readers the option of not getting your e-mails in the
future. The unsubscribe option is also a message reinforcing the
idea that they want to get your e-mails.

Model copy is "You can unsubscribe anytime. To unsubscribe,
(directions)..."

5. Email 2-3 times

The standard appears to be sending the e-mail out 2-3 times to a
given person for an upcoming session of courses, event, or other
major activity. Space your e-mail notices out over a period of weeks.

6. Subject line should be the same

To create familiarity and get higher readership, the Subject line
of your e-mails should always be the same.

7. Email same time of month

The more regular your e-mails, the more you create anticipation
and receptivity. The ideal is to e-mail the same week of the month,
same day of the week, and even the same time of day.

8. Track as much as possible

Track the effectiveness of your e-mails. Keep track of these rates:

- Bounce, or do not get through to the intended recipient.
- Open, or how many of the e-mails sent actually get opened.
- Click through rate, or how many of the e-mail recipients click on a link for more information or registration.

9. Update e-mail addresses

Like snail mail addresses, e-mail addresses get out of date. For your past participants, it is worth your time and effort to get updated e-mail addresses when your e-mails bounce back.

10. Do not spam

When someone gives your program their e-mail address, they are giving you permission to e-mail them. You should send e-mails your past participants and those people who have inquired about your program.

But do not spam. Spam is when you get a list of e-mail addresses who are not your customers and you start e-mailing the people without their permission. If you get an e-mail list, use it only once and invite recipients to sign up if they want additional e-mails.

Chapter 11
Needs Assessment

Why Needs Assessment Has Become So Important

Professionals with lifelong learning programs are increasingly becoming interested in needs assessment — finding out what their participants, customers, and members want. There is a good and significant reason why more professionals are focusing their attention on needs assessment these days.

The world of lifelong learning has been revised totally in the last few years. No longer can programs offer products — courses, seminars, events, classes, etc. — and expect that people will come.

The learner is now determining what she or he wants to learn, and when, and how. And with increasing market segmentation, there is no one audience out there for our programs. There are many audiences. Each audience may want something different.

The job of professionals in lifelong learning has changed. It used to be to offer educational activities and to get people to come to those programs. Today the job is to determine what learners want and then to create those educational activities around the needs of the audience being served.

With that fundamental shift, needs assessments have moved to the top of the list of priorities and job function for more and more programmers.

Another reason needs assessment has become more important today is that the key to programming success is no longer to find a program that has been popular or successful elsewhere and to offer it.

Where to find the model

Shown on the next page, the 8-stage model is fully explained in LERN's publication *Successful Needs Assessments*. Various aspects of the model have been explored in LERN's *Developing Successful New Programs* manual. And articles on needs assessment have appeared in our newsletters and magazine over the past several years. On the Internet, you can look up the Program Development section of the LERN Library in the LERN Club and view and download many reports on the subject.

Needs assessment now a process

With all the market segmentation, competition and changing learner needs in our industry, there are few if any easy, standard "answers" to programming success. Instead, the answers are unique to your individual program and audience. Thus, there are no longer any blanket answers useful for all programs. Instead, there is a process by which you can determine what works for your audience.

Historically, most professionals in lifelong learning just tried a new activity, course, or event. "You never know what works" has been one long cherished view and common phrase. "Just go on your hunch" has been another.

In the last few years professionals have tried to enhance new program success by surveying participants and even non-participants. While surveying participants is an important part of the process, it is only ONE stage in the process of good needs assessment.

Costs and risks have increased

Another reason for more needs assessments today is that the risks have increased for offering new activities, and the costs for failing with new programs is growing. Professionals now understand the concept of lifetime value, and that success with a new audience or program can result in high income over a three-year period. Failing initially can mean losing that income totally.

Staff time has also become more valuable. With high-dollar programs, it is now more cost effective to do a good needs assessment and succeed with a new program than to just try it and risk the high cost of failure.

LERN's 8-Stage Needs Assessment Model

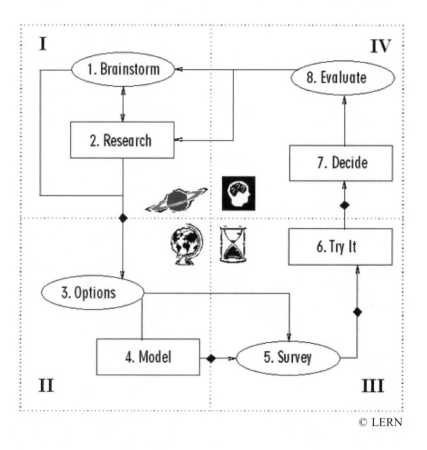

Overview of the 8-Stage Model

The 8 stages of the new needs assessment model are:

1. Brainstorming. Gathering 10-20 ideas from all sources, including staff and participants. No idea is a bad idea. It is a critical first step without which the other stages cannot succeed.

2. Research. At the same time you are doing brainstorming, you are also doing research. This includes data and numbers on your current participants and activities, analyzing the competition, and reviewing the total environment.

3. Selecting Options. From all the ideas brainstormed and researched, you narrow your choices down to 2-3 options. A small group such as an advisory board, focus group or leadership council is very helpful in this process.

4. Modeling. A critical stage is working out a potential new program on paper. Without putting some numbers to paper, such as response rate, cost of promotion and production, anticipated participants, and so on, it is difficult if not impossible to succeed.

5. Survey. At this stage, you survey a section of your participants to gain additional and final information on what will make the program a success.

6. Try it. After going through five stages, you try the new idea by offering it to your audience and giving it your best promotional shot. If you have spent enough time and thought on the first five stages, this effort should provide evidence that the new program will be successful over the long term.

7. Decide. Often times not enough energy and thought is put into analyzing the results of the first effort. Sometimes new programs are killed when they actually have demonstrated long-term success, even though the first program may not have made money.

8. Evaluate. Every program needs ongoing evaluation to improve it. Certainly all new programs will need to be refined and tuned to improve the quality and the profitability.

Successful Strategies for Needs Assessment

In the context of this publication, needs assessment is "an ongoing process of discovering what your program's participants want in terms of activities and services."

What Needs Assessment Is NOT
- It's not expensive.
- It's not a one-time study.
- It's not more work — it replaces wasted staff time and its results maximize profits and services.
- It's not a general overview — it is very specific.
- It's not the same as environmental scanning, though it can be used in environmental scanning.
- It's not something you contract out; it is too important; it is something you and your staff do.

What Needs Assessment IS
- It is customer oriented.
- It is low cost.
- It involves some or all of your staff in some way.
- It is ongoing.
- It does not separate 'needs' from 'wants.'
- It understands that the participants or customers know more about their needs than any other entity.
- It is practical.
- It costs less than not doing needs assessments.

Who Does Needs Assessments

Programmers do needs assessments. Needs assessments should not be contracted out. They should not be delegated to support staff. They should not be conducted solely by the marketing staff, although the marketing staff should be doing its own needs assessments.

"Programmers" are lifelong learning professionals who design courses, seminars, events, classes, conferences, or activities. They line up instructors or teachers, select times, find places, and often are involved in writing copy for the brochure.

Programmers today have to be involved — immersed, rather — in needs assessment in order for their activities (classes, seminars, etc.) to be successful. It used to be that programmers could line up activities and then go out and recruit people to attend. That model, a product-based model, no longer works.

Today the model that works is a customer-oriented, learner-centered, market-focused model. Activities are designed around your participants, your customers' needs. We cannot approach programming today by saying, "Here is our activity. How do we get people to come to it?" Instead, we have to say, "Here is our audience. How do we design activities they will want to attend?"

Thus, needs assessments are central to programming success. Programmers cannot know what topics to offer, nor how to offer them (time, place, etc.) without doing needs assessments. That is why programmers should be doing needs assessments.

The High Cost of Not Doing Needs Assessments

There are many reasons why needs assessment is a hot topic among lifelong learning professionals today. But the bottom line reason is that it costs more not to do needs assessments today than it costs to do them.

Twenty years ago, lifelong learning programs offered activities based on staff opinion, often called "hunches." "You never know what works; you have to go on your hunch" was a typical comment. Ten years ago, programs started surveying their participants, and within the last several years have found that that approach alone is not very helpful either. These other approaches — using your best guess, doing surveys, or even asking an advisory council, turn out to have a higher cost, not a lower cost, than doing comprehensive ongoing needs assessments.

If you do not do needs assessments, several serious consequences will result:

A. You will incur a higher failure rate than is necessary or even tolerable.

Based on our years of experience and consulting, we have determined that a national "failure rate" for lifelong learning activities is around 25 percent. About 25 percent of the typical program's activities are losers. They do not even cover direct costs (in addition, other activities may cover direct costs, but not indirect costs). That means about 25 percent of your staff's time is wasted. It takes just as much staff time and organizational money to line up and promote a losing activity as it does to line up and promote a winning activity.

Needs assessments will cut your failure rate so much that the staff time involved in doing needs assessments will more than be made up by the higher success rate of your activities.

B. You will lose audiences.

There's something even more costly than the staff time and money involved in offering losing activities. That is the cost in losing audiences, your market segments. When you offer losing activities, you don't just lose money. You also lose customers and participants.

Individual customers and participants have a lifetime value that far exceeds a single activity. When you lose a customer, you lose three to five times your typical fee. When you lose enough customers or participants, you lose a whole market segment, a whole audience.

It is extremely hard to get a whole audience back. For example, if you start to do activities for nurses, and your first few activities are losers, you could lose the whole nursing market for your program.

C. You will lose future success to your competition.

Needs assessments are not just valuable in determining your next offerings, they are also central to exploring and creating future activities. If you do not know the needs of your participants, your competition will step in and discover their needs. And then you will lose your participants to your competition. It is no longer good enough to stay even with your participants. To be successful in the future, to stay ahead of the competition, you now need to stay ahead of your participants.

Research High-Dollar Programs

Needs assessments should be done for high-dollar programs. Some examples are:
- Starting computer classes
- A conference
- Doing seminars for a new target audience
- Classes for children
- A certificate program

All of the above examples can probably generate at least $100,000 or more over a three-year period. This potential for $100,000 in income over a three-year period should be a rough benchmark as to whether to devote time and energy to a needs assessment.

This publication is written specifically for high-dollar efforts, those that have the most impact on your program and on your bottom line.

Some low-dollar activities for which it would not be cost effective to do too much needs assessment:
- Individual sessions at a conference
- One-time offerings
- A single class or course

For these low-dollar activities, follow these guidelines:
1. Accept a normal cancellation or failure rate, based on your historical experience. For example, if 33 percent of your new classes fail, accept that failure rate and base your calculations and projections on this rate.
2. Look at a larger group or division. For example, if you are trying out a new computer class, look at how well all the computer classes do as a whole.

3. Do quick surveys. Quick surveys might help, might not. For example, for individual sessions at your annual conference, a survey of past attendees about future sessions is one indication of potential.
4. Just do it.

With low-dollar activities, such as an individual class or a one-hour workshop at your conference, there are many fluctuations and variables involved. And because they are very low dollar, devoting time and resources to an individual low-dollar activity is not cost effective for your organization. Look at "divisions" or groups of activities. A division is a much higher-dollar activity, so using the needs assessment model is quite effective and profitable.

Three Central Uses of Needs Assessments

The needs assessment process can be used in many ways. But there are at least three central uses of needs assessments from which your organization can profit substantially.

1. Determining which customers to serve

The biggest and highest dollar usage of needs assessments is to determine which customers to serve. This is also where your best opportunity for organizational growth exists.

Your customers or participants fall into various market segments. Your programs serves many different market segments, or audiences (groups of people). But you do not serve them all equally, and only seven market segments give you 80 percent of your income.

Yet even those seven market segments do not stay static. Even your best market segments are changing over time, the course of three to five years. Some market segments are growing. Some are not growing. One or two may be declining. And there are one to five market segments not currently in your top seven which might be able to be stimulated to become one of your best market segments.

Exploring which market segments (examples: nurses, rural residents, older adults, children, executives with companies of more than 100 employees, etc.) to pursue, and which ones not to pursue, is probably the most high-dollar usage of needs assessments. Using the 8-Stage Needs Assessment Model, you can research new markets and audiences to determine which ones to pursue.

2. Determining what activities to offer

Once you have found which market segments to serve, you need to know what activities (courses, seminars, classes, events, etc.) to offer. This is the most common use of needs assessments, and a good one. Using the 8-Stage Needs Assessment Model, you can increase your program's rate of new activity success.

3. Determining how your activities should be offered

No longer is the topic the only motivating factor in getting participants to your program. There are also other considerations in whether people will come, and thus whether your new activity will be a success or not.

Some of those other "how" factors include time, place, instructors, price and promotion. Getting the best information possible on all of these factors is a third positive use of needs assessments.

All of these uses of needs assessments have practical, bottom-line outcomes for the success of your programs and activities. Needs assessment is not just a project for long-term planning, an overview for the public or media, or wishful daydreaming. Needs assessments are central, critical functions that lead directly to program success.

Chapter 12
Program Development

Determining Objectives

In tough economic times, program managers need to use every option available to maximize enrollment in classes. In the current economic climate, realizing the highest possible enrollment per class offered is a serious goal. There are some simple planning techniques that can help achieve this goal.

Determine Income Objective. The first thing to do is look at the budget for the year. For example, if the budget is $378,000 then this becomes the income goal for the program. If your program offers six sessions per year, you know that each session needs to generate $63,000 in order to meet this goal.

In reality, your experience may tell you that this is unrealistic. For example, your July/August session may not have the potential to generate this kind of income. In that case, you need to look at each session independently, determine a realistic income goal based on past experience, and make sure the total projected for all your sessions realistically equals your budget goal.

Determine Enrollment Objective. To do this, you will need to use data from past sessions to determine your average class fee. This number is the average amount that a participant pays to take a class. To derive this figure simply divide your last session's (or last year's) income by the total number of registrations for that session or year. Do not include those registrations that were in canceled classes or who subsequently withdrew and received a refund.

In the budget example we are using, if you determine your average class fee to be $28, you would divide $63,000 by $28 and learn that you will need 2,250 registrations to meet your budget goal.

Determine Number of Courses. Now you are ready to figure out how many participants you average per course. To do this divide your last session's (or last year's) registrations by the number of courses. Let's assume that you determine that you average 10 participants per class. To generate 2,250 registrations, then, you will need 225 successful classes.

Keep in mind your cancellation rate when determining a final figure for the number of classes to offer. Again, use the experience of the past to estimate your cancellation rate. If your cancellation rate normally runs around 20 percent, you should add another 45 classes so you end up offering 270 courses. After cancellations, you will have 225 successful classes and a good chance of getting the enrollments you need.

Determine Categories of Courses. Before starting to recruit teachers, look at the categories of courses you are offering by session. You know you want to offer 270 classes, but the question is now, how do you maximize the enrollment potential of these classes?

If you look in the category of fine arts and determine that you typically generate only five percent of your enrollment in this area, you will not want to offer a high percentage of your total class offerings in this area. If, on the other hand, your fine arts classes generate 35 percent of your enrollment, you would want to offer a higher percentage of courses in this area.

Look at the average enrollments in your arts classes. Then divide the number of enrollments by the average per class in this section.

For example, 35 percent or 787 enrollments occur in the fine arts section. With an average of 15 enrollments per class, you would want to plan on a minimum of 52 classes (about 20 percent of total) in the fine arts section to achieve this enrollment objective.

If this is a real "bread-and-butter" section, producing higher than average enrollments per class and a high percentage of total class enrollments, you might want to offer more classes in this area, since it is proven to be attractive to your audience.

These steps are simple, and the data needed to develop a solid plan is available in every program. They come directly from your enrollment records. By following this step-by-step process, you can have greater confidence that the work you are doing will have the highest likelihood of producing the number of enrollments you need.

Reasons to Create New Programs

There are seven reasons to create new programs. When developing new courses/seminars, check this list to see if you are doing so for one or more of these reasons. If you are not, you should closely evaluate your reason.

1. Generate New Sales. Add dollars to total income. Certain divisions are lacking programs and need to be beefed up. Many times failing to look at numbers means we miss out on targeting programs that can be expanded.

2. Increase Operating Margin. Your present mix of programs may not be generating the operating margin you need. They may be popular, but the cost may be too high or the price too low. Developing new programs with a better operating margin can increase your present operating margin. You may choose to price these programs higher or reduce costs. Even if this is what you are already doing, be aware that too many programs with a low operating margin could truly jeopardize the future of your total program.

3. Build Customer Base. By offering more new programs, you may do a better job of targeting segments that are not being served appropriately and you might just reach out to people not currently involved with your program. A diverse, but not overextended, selection can be helpful in adding new names to your database.

4. Keep Catalog/Promotions Fresh and Current. Many times customers move on to another organization because there aren't enough new products to choose from. Also, many times potential customers do not even review a program if they feel it is just a rehash of what came across their desk six months earlier. It is important to be always adding new, so that the public feels that you are spending energy and time listening and responding. As stated earlier, it is all a perception. Image is everything.

5. Energize and Challenge Staff. Programming staff can fall into easy routines quickly. If they are not being challenged to develop new products, they will do what is easy. Also, if they are not made accountable for the products they develop, they will not look to add new programs.

6. Respond to Customer Needs. The customer is the boss. If the customers are looking for new programs, it is our responsibility to give them what they want.

7. Cut Out Losers. Since there is only so much promotional space, developing new programs will probably force the elimination of programs that are not carrying their own weight. This is important, because many times losers are left in way too long and weigh down all of our hard work.

Where to Expand

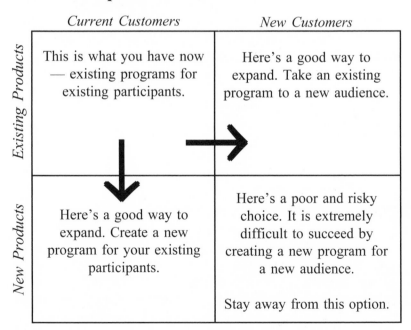

	Current Customers	*New Customers*
Existing Products	This is what you have now — existing programs for existing participants.	Here's a good way to expand. Take an existing program to a new audience.
New Products	Here's a good way to expand. Create a new program for your existing participants.	Here's a poor and risky choice. It is extremely difficult to succeed by creating a new program for a new audience. Stay away from this option.

Challenges of Creating New Programs

As we will find as we explore the specific strategies and tools for developing new programs, doing this job right takes dedication, concentration and a lot of hard work. You cannot just sit in your office and only dream or just wait for new programs to come knocking on the door. You need to be actively engaged in a process that has specific steps, tools, and strategies.

LERN recommends that every program offer 20% to 30% new activities or offerings each year. New offerings are now critical to maintain the vitality and viability of your programming. Offer a minimum of 20%, and a maximum of 30%, new offerings each year.

The Ten Right Questions of Success

A step-by-step model for planning new programs

There are ten "right" questions to ask your participants before developing a successful new program. Getting answers to these questions can dramatically increase the success rate of your new programs.

Without knowing much about what your audience wants, your chances for success with your hunch, your thoughts, and with trial and error are very low. But after you ask your audience LERN's Ten Right Questions, your chances of success go up significantly.

Here are the ten right questions to ask:

1. Is this the right audience?

You ask this question indirectly of your participants, not in a survey questionnaire. You find out the total universe for the audience. You find out whether you can get or create a mailing list of this audience. You find out if they are already served in the same way by another program.

This is the most important question. Because if you are trying to reach an audience that is not right for your program, there is nothing you can do to make it the right audience. The right topic, format, time, day and so on all cannot change things if you do not have the right audience. So make sure this is a good audience for your program.

2. Is this the right subject area?

You can survey your participants directly about what subject areas they are most interested in.

Subject area interest is going to change over time for the same audience. It is certainly going to vary when you try to serve a different audience or market segment. So knowing what subject area your audience is most interested in is very important.

3. Is this the right topic?

This is not the same as the right subject. Within any given subject area, there are many topics. Just because a person is interested in "management" or "environment" does not mean that any topic in a subject area will meet the audience's needs. So after you survey for subject, survey for topic.

4. Is this the right title?

Again, this is not the same as the right topic. Any topic can be offered using a variety of different program titles. Some titles will be a smash hit; some titles will be a flop. Survey your participants for the right title for your new program.

5. Is this the right format?

There is no longer one format that is appropriate for all your various market segments or audiences. And the same audience may want a different format for a particular subject.

Look at all the available formats, then look at all the available terms for formats.

6. Is this the right place?

Once again, variety and choice are the keys to success with programming, so do not take the location for granted. Maybe a new site would make a critical difference for the audience.

7. Is this the right time?

Every audience has different time constraints. For some audiences, the time of day is important. For others the day of the week is important. For others, the week of the month. And for others the month of the year. So confirm that the time you have chosen is one that is optimal for your audience.

8. Is this the right instructor?

For some programs, the type of instructor may make a difference in your attendance figures. Look at various options for your instructor/s or program leader/s. You can have an expert, an outside expert, a peer, and so on.

9. Is this the right price?

This you can best discover only indirectly or by conducting a price test with your audience. Asking your audience their best price is unlikely to be helpful. Few people will tell you a program is too inexpensive.

10. Is this the right promotion?

This can best be discovered indirectly. You can ask a focus group to give you feedback on two different kinds of promotional packages. For example, you can ask them which brochure is more attractive to them. You can also look at other types of promotions to the audience you are trying to reach. And, depending on the dollar value of the new program, you can also do a promotional test and see which of two packages pulls better for you.

Product Life Span

Too often we take on more than we can handle. By not focusing our efforts, we do too much and we do not do it well. We try to be everything to too many people. Normally these people are not in our top seven segments and ultimately people we are spending a great deal of money on for very little pay back.

Knowing your USP is important in solving this problem. Knowing your segments is important. A few other important points are:

- You do not always need to be first. Sometimes it is appropriate to watch the competition and learn what worked and failed for them before you jump in feet first.

- Often we offer too many products. This is sometimes true in divisions and with segments that are our most popular. We need to be careful to offer only as much as the market can absorb. Sometimes we need to rest products instead of continually running them. Having too much line expansion can exhaust resources and overwhelm staff.
- Tracking the life of your products is a key task. By tracking the life of your product you can better determine when to pull a product and also when to offer a new product that your customers will be willing and ready to register for.

In tracking the life of your product, a tool that can be used is the "S" Curve. The number of registrations, the total income, and the operating margin are performance indicators that dictate how well the course/seminar has done.

1. Registrations. How many people have signed up each time the course/seminar has been offered?
2. Income. How much total income has been generated each time the course/seminar has been offered?
3. Operating Margin. What is the operating margin percentage and dollar amount after deducting promotion and production costs from the total income?

Each of these three areas can be graphed, so that you can evaluate past performance and predict what will happen in the future. Many times just knowing this information will help you make minor adjustments that can improve overall performance.

A. If registrations are strong, but operating margin is weak, you can most certainly increase the price of the course/seminar.
B. If the operating margin is good, but the total income is low, you may decide to spend more money on promotion.

When evaluating your information, you may find it helpful to use the "S" Curve method. The "S" Curve is a great tool for tracking product life, as well as a stimulant for making decisions about adding new programs or eliminating new or old programs.

The "S" Curve has four sections:

- Section 1 is the period of time when a new product is introduced. Normally the product will generate a reasonable

The "S" Curve

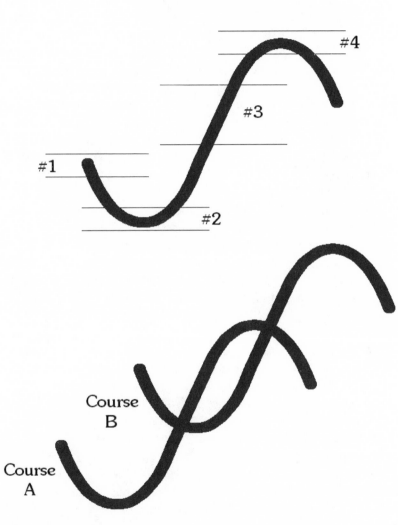

response (covers direct costs: promotion and production) if you have done the necessary needs assessments work prior to introducing the product. If the response does not at least cover promotion and production costs, you should make a quick decision about running the course/seminar in the future.

- Section 2 is the period of time when the response to the product may dip. This is normally because those initially involved have not had time to spread the word or those who take longer to respond are not yet ready to register. Doing a better job of promoting the course/seminar by using database information from the first group will help eliminate the dip. Don't be afraid of a dip, but be aware that more targeted promotion is probably necessary.

- Section 3 is the period of time when the product is receiving the most attention. People are responding strongly because of your promotion or word of mouth. This is the time when you need to start developing your next course or seminar for this group of participants. This should be the beginning of "S" Curve number two: a new course or event that is developed particularly for this group's interest. This may be the offering of a more advanced program or a supporting or spin-off program.

- Section 4 is when you should be looking to pull the course or seminar. The numbers are starting to dip and it is better to pull a course or seminar before it bottoms out. If you wait until this time to develop new programs, you may miss attracting your most interested customers, the people who have recently participated in the course or seminar.

Using the "S" Curve to graph and track the registration numbers, dollars, and operating margin is a simple visual tool. Most important, Section 3 of the "S" Curve alerts programmers to when they should be introducing new courses or seminars.

Chapter 13
Program Analysis

Key Formulas

There are four key formulas that are critical in analyzing and projecting enrollments and income. They are applicable to any kind of lifelong learning program with open enrollments (that is, promoted and marketed to an audience).

The first key formula is Average Participants per Class.

$$\text{Average Participants per Class/Event} = \frac{\text{\# Registrations}}{\text{\# Events}}$$

This is the average number of people in a given class or course. This figure is the number of enrollments divided by the number of classes.

An enrollment and registration are the same thing: one person taking one activity or class. If one person takes two classes, it is two enrollments.

For example, if we had 1,000 people and 2,500 registrations for 250 classes, our Average Participants Per Class would be 10.

The second key formula is Average Class Fee.

$$\text{Average Class/Event Fee} = \frac{\text{\$ Income}}{\text{\# Registrations}}$$

This is the average or typical class fee. It is the total income for a session or year divided by the number of enrollments. It is NOT the income an average class generates. It is the average registration fee.

For example, if we had $60,000 in income and 2,000 enrollments, our Average Class Fee would be $30.

These two formulas are central to your financial planning. You want to know your average participants per class for your program as a whole, and then for each Division within your program.

The same is true with your average class fee. You want to know the average class fee for your total program, and for each Division within your program.

The third key formula is the Course Cancellation Rate.

$$\text{Course Cancellation Rate} = \frac{\text{\# Cancelled Events}}{\text{\# Events Offered}}$$

This is how many classes you cancel, on the average. You find it by dividing the number of cancelled classes by the number of classes offered.

For example, if you offered 200 classes and cancelled 20, your cancellation rate would be 10%.

Again, this figure should be determined for your overall program and for each Division.

The fourth key formula is your Brochure:Participant Ratio.

$$\text{Brochure : Participant Ratio} = \frac{\text{\# Brochures Distributed}}{\text{\# Registrations}}$$

This is how many brochures it takes to get one registration. Again it is registration, not person.

To find the number, divide the total number of brochures distributed by the number of enrollments. You can do this by session or by year.

If you are doing direct mail exclusively, and are involved with courses for business or continuing professional development, you may want to think of this number as your Response Rate. This is the same as Brochure: Participant Ratio, just expressed as a percentage.

$$\text{Response Rate} = \frac{\text{\# Registrations}}{\text{\# Brochures Distributed}}$$

If we distribute 200,000 brochures and get 5,000 enrollments, our Brochure: Participant Ratio is 40:1. Expressed as a Response Rate, the Response Rate would be 2.5%.

If you combine all your classes and courses into one brochure, you would have one figure for all your classes and courses. However, if you promote various Divisions with separate brochures or additional promotion, you can also analyze this figure by Division.

All four key formulas can be analyzed by session or by year. And another level of sophistication is to analyze each by the season or session of the year, because the figures may very well change from your fall session to your winter session, from spring to summer.

With these key formulas, you can predict your enrollments and income.

Cancellation Rate Analysis

Another increasingly important financial tool is cancellation rate analysis.

As the chart on the next page shows, successful programs have a mix of between 70% and 90% old courses, with the rest being new courses. More than 90% old courses means you don't have enough new courses. With less than 70% old courses, you have too many risky new courses. (An "old course" is one that has been offered successfully the previous session. A "new course" is one that has not been offered successfully within the last few years.)

Because new courses cancel in much higher proportions than old courses, the acceptable cancellation rate for each is different. That allows you to cancel 30% to 50%, one third to one half, of your new courses and still have a successful offering.

For old courses, you want to keep the cancellation rate as low as possible.

The ideal course cancellation rate overall is 15%.

This is another tool for financial analysis. Use cancellation rate analysis to analyze your courses by Division as well, zeroing in on where the problems are.

Course* Cancellation Rates

	% of Classes Offered	Acceptable Cancellation Rate	% Cancelled of Total
Old Courses	70% - 90%	0 - 13%	0 - 12%
New Courses	30% - 10%	50% - 30%	15% - 3%
Total	100%	——	15%

* Cancellation rate for seminars & conferences = 0%

Chapter 14
Pricing

Listing Your Prices

How we list our prices does have an effect on attendance. Here are some guidelines:

1.Do not put decimals and zeros after the price. For example, do NOT list a price as $195.00. List it as $195.

2.In listings, avoid round numbers. In an informal survey of association-sponsored seminars and conferences, we found about half used round numbers, such as $50, $100, or $200 for their fees. There are two things that go on with round numbers. One, you are more apt to hit a price break if you list your prices in round numbers. And two, people just don't like to buy things priced in round numbers.

People like to buy things whose prices end in 5 and 9, say pricing experts. Instead of listing your price as $50, list it as $45, $49 or $59.

3.Don't highlight, and don't hide, your price. Generally, price is not a reason for a person to attend your event, so highlighting your fee is not recommended. The exception is if your event has a lot of competition and you are offering it at an extremely low price as compared to the competition.

On the other hand, you should not hide your price either. It should be located at the back of your brochure or publicity, but people should be able to find the price easily. To make it difficult to find is to give the impression that you are trying to conceal it.

Playing Price Breaks

A strange phenomenon in consumer purchasing is called the "price break," the point at which a person says the price is too high. Different people have different price breaks, and of course there are separate price breaks of various kinds for seminars and conferences.

Some price breaks are $25, $50, $100, $200, $500 and $1,000. The larger the number, the less often there is a price break. For prices under $100, $25 is a price break and so is $50. But a fee of $225 is probably not a price break in the $200-$300 price range, while $250 might be. And $550 is probably not a price break in the over-$500 price range.

We are all influenced by price breaks. The fee of $100 is a price break for some of us. For my staff, for example, $100 is a price break. If there is a seminar for $98 and a staff person wants to attend, I would approve it. I usually say, "Go, you need this, take some notes, have a good time." For the same seminar priced at $102, my reaction is, "We're not IBM. We don't have that kind of money to throw around."

Price as Image

We also have a concept of people attending events at various price levels. While it is fine to send support staff, for instance, to seminars priced at under $100, administrators and executives are less likely to attend. We just don't feel that there can be that much in it to learn at that price. But if the same event, the same speaker is priced at $195, we will attend.

This has been shown to be the case with computer seminars. Price the computer seminar at $45 and certain types of people will attend. Take the same seminar with the same speaker and description, and price it at $195 and other types of people will attend. And they both will evaluate the seminar without regard to price, but on the merits of the content.

So we have an image of seminars and conferences, and the price of a particular event is part of our image of it. Association expert Jim Lowe said that we are what we are perceived to be. That is certainly true in terms of prices. We convey an image in our pricing.

A very low price is going to indicate a lack of quality to some people, while most of us assume a high-priced event is of high quality. While this is not always true, it is the case in enough instances that most of us relate price to quality.

Underpricing

Most of us are concerned about raising prices so high that we turn attendees away. In fact, the most common mistake in pricing seminars and conferences, according to seminar guru Anver Suleiman, is underpricing — charging too little.

The concepts of price breaks and price as image means that some of us will not spend over a certain amount to attend an event. But it also means that we will not spend less than a certain amount to attend an event.

There is an actual perfect case study of underpricing from a town in British Columbia, told to me by one of the people involved during a seminar I conducted near Victoria.

In this town, three different organizations contracted with the same speaker to give the same seminar, with each organization unaware that the speaker was contracted with either of the other agencies. One priced the seminar at $35. Another priced it at $95. And the third priced it at $135. The title, speaker, and brochure copy were identical.

The program that offered the seminar at $35 had to cancel for lack of enrollments. The program that offered it at $95 was three-quarters full. And the program that offered the seminar at $135 had a waiting list and had to turn people away.

It is not only possible to underprice, it happens all the time and it happens more frequently than overpricing. Underpricing has the same negative effect on attendance as overpricing — it turns people away.

The Impact of Pricing on Attendance

It is commonly assumed that an increase in price is accompanied by a decrease in attendance. That is not true in most cases.

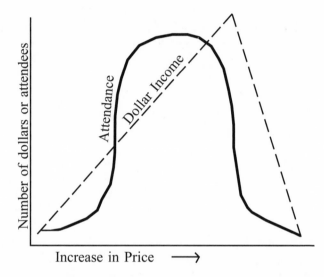

This is a chart of the effect of price on attendance. There is a rough correlation between the two, but it is not what is commonly assumed. On the chart, we start with a price of zero and increase the price along the horizontal axis. The resulting impact on attendance and on income is shown on the vertical axis. The attendance curve shows that attendance actually increases for a while when we raise prices. Income also increases with the price increase, as attendance increases. After a certain point attendance does not increase as the price increases, but it does not decrease either. It remains stable. Income, however, continues to grow as a result of the price increase and stabilized attendance. If we continue to raise the price, eventually the attendance will drop but the income will continue to grow or remain stable. Finally, if we increase the price enough, a sharp decrease in attendance follows, and thus a decrease in income. That stage is the one we all fear, but one that happens infrequently. Instead, most of us are somewhere else on the chart, which means that increasing prices would be beneficial rather than detrimental.

Chapter 15
Program Management

The Ideal Staffing Structure

A redesigned lifelong learning program must have a staffing structure that is streamlined and clearly understood. Staff members need to know what their responsibilities are, and they must be willing to work as a team with other staff. Each person is an important cog in the wheel and must feel important but also must be accountable for his/her performance.

For the past several years, LERN has been describing a staffing structure that has included three components, CEO/director, programming, and operations. During the past year or so, two more components, marketing and sales, have been added. These new components have evolved because marketing has become more complex and because the need for contract training by businesses and organizations has exploded.

This new staffing structure is being embraced by associations, recreation departments, colleges and universities, and all other types of lifelong learning programs. The structure has evolved from the successful experiences of for-profit businesses and has been tested by independent lifelong learning programs, both for profit and non-profit. The following are the five components of this staffing structure.

CEO/Director — The CEO/director is the leader of the lifelong learning program. He/she is the visionary who is in touch with what is going on in the field and is committed to the program's mission, vision, values and Unique Selling Proposition.

The key responsibility of this position is marketing. This "high-dollar" work is done by reaching into the program's community and searching for new market and product opportunities. Opportunities are then brought back to the rest of the program to test, develop and implement.

At the same time, the CEO/director needs to focus his/her time on staff development. He/she wants to have the most knowledgeable and capable staff possible.

As the leader of the lifelong learning program, the CEO/director manages the Operations Professional, the Marketing Professional, the Sales Professional and the Programming Professional, his/her management team, and together this team makes sure that the program's one-year marketing plan is followed and other policy decisions are made.

The CEO/director's job involves environmental scanning, testing, research, analyzing the competition, financial and budgetary skills, reams of paper with statistics from the program, and listening.

Programming Professional — The Programming Professional and his/her staff are primarily responsible for the development of new products for present customers and selecting existing products for new markets.

The programming staff should not be involved in the day-to-day operations of the lifelong learning program. They need to be given the time to research, test and develop. The most successful programmers are those that manage customers and not products. Programmers accountable for a segment of customers are able to spend time talking to, surveying and learning from customers so they can better develop and price courses/events that will generate registrations.

Thus, the programmers must be accountable for numbers. They need to be able to justify their selections by predicting the final registration, income, operating margin and quality performance and by recommending specific marketing strategies learned while interacting with his/her customer segment. Instructors are accountable to programmers. Programmers hire, fire, evaluate, train and negotiate with instructors.

Programmers also work directly with sales professionals when contracts are developed. The sales professional "opens the door," but the programmers work with the sales professional and client to develop a product that best meets the client's need.

Critical activities of a programmer are market research, market data collection, including extensive data collection on customer demographics and purchasing history, customer and target audience research, marketing strategies, planning, new product development, initial instructor recruitment, budgeting and analysis.

Operations Professional — The Operations Professional and his/her staff are primarily responsible for the day-to-day management of the lifelong learning program. While the programmers focus on customer management, the operations staff focus on customer service.

Areas include registration, promotion production and distribution, bookkeeping and refunds, management information services (reports), logistics such as room setup, tabulating course/event evaluations, scheduling repeat instructors for future teaching slots and other routine activities.

Most support staff are members of the operations staff. The Operations Professional is responsible for coordinating staff and setting priorities, as well as contracting out work that can be better done by someone not on staff.

An important position on the operations staff is the Information Specialist. This person is the primary contact for customers with questions or problems. The Information Specialist is trained to answer most questions and if he/she does not know the answer, he/she can contact the appropriate programmer for the answer. The Information Specialist is also given the authority to make refund decisions and other decisions that will give a customer an immediate answer.

A lifelong learning program with limited operations problems and challenges is better poised to grow. The Operations Professional is responsible for eliminating operations headaches, as well as supplying the rest of the program with information that can be used when making decisions.

Marketing Professional — The Marketing Professional is responsible for "think marketing." He/she is the one who develops marketing strategies that are implemented by the operations staff. Like the programmers, he/she is not involved in the day-to-day operations of the program.

Since marketing is everything we do, it has become a much more complex responsibility. The Marketing Professional is responsible for the program's image, as well as selecting mailing lists and deciding the number of promotions to print.

A key component of the job is looking at purchasing history and key demographic statistics. The Marketing Professional is the person who develops and tracks the program's market segments, making sure that the proper resources are being spent on the segments that are most valuable to the program.

He/she is also responsible for the design of the program's brochure and other promotional efforts. Whether the materials are printed or on the web site, the Marketing Professional is responsible for the image and message being sent to customers and non-customers.

Under the direction of the CEO/director, the Marketing Professional develops the program's one-year marketing plan. This is done in coordination with the other professionals, but it is his/her responsibility to get the plan produced on time. It is also his/her responsibility to get the one-year marketing plan end-of-year report completed.

This is a new position, but one that will make an enormous difference to a lifelong learning program. We do not think about marketing enough, and this position has the luxury to do just that, as well as to test various promotion options.

Sales Professional — The Sales Professional is responsible for selling contracts. This person is a salesperson who directly works with clients to sell contracts that meet the clients' needs/wants.

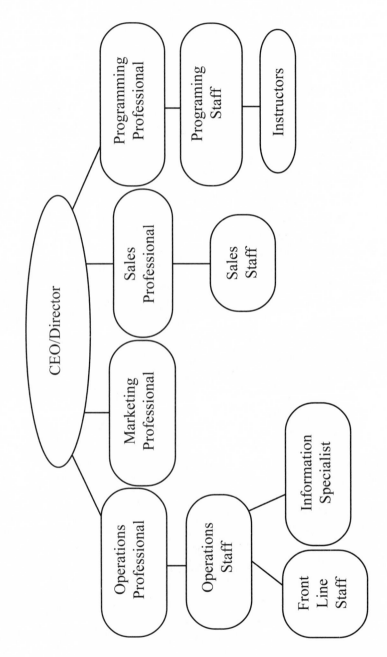

Ideal Staffing Structure

The Sales Professional is in the business of relationship selling. He/she needs to be meeting with clients, explaining the capabilities of the lifelong learning program and developing a relationship based on trust. Most contracts are sold on the merits of the salesperson and not the perceived merits of the product.

The Sales Professional's duties require him/her to develop a relationship with both the programming and operations staffs. He/she makes the initial client contact and then works with the programming staff developing a product. Once the contract is signed, he/she works with the operations staff to implement the contract. The Sales Professional is not a product developer, although he/she is capable of explaining product options, and he/she is not the person who monitors each contract. He/she must be freed up to continue to make contacts for future business.

A Sales Professional can do initial client needs assessments, as well as quality assurance audits at the completion of the contract. This person must be organized and must keep good records of past purchases, as well as needs/wants.

Development Priorities

Having these five staffing structure components would be very beneficial to your lifelong learning program. Many programs are too small for this staffing structure, but you can grow into this staffing structure. It is most important to realize that these tasks must be separated. Look at your present staff and you may find that you can make some immediate responsibility changes that better focus staff energies.

The following are five steps you can take in adapting to this staffing structure:

1. Get the CEO/director out of the day-to-day. He/she should be out developing new income opportunities — income opportunities that will allow you to grow your business and staff.
2. Find a person who has the capabilities of being the Operations Professional. This is not an easy job. It requires a person who can juggle many balls at one time. Let him/her start

absorbing various routine operations activities that are now being handled in the programming area.

3. Reduce the size of your programming staff. If your programming staff is primarily responsible for developing 20–30% new programs a year, you do not need as many people. Move them to the operations staff where they are really needed.

4. Add a Sales Professional. Start selling contracts. They are profitable, and they are great for your image.

5. Add a Marketing Professional. Once all the other pieces are in place, you are ready to assign a person to "think marketing."

What All Staff Should Understand

In the future, lifelong learning will continue to become more and more central to every adult's life. But meeting the needs of adults has become more complicated, and the demands on lifelong learning programs have grown. Challenges cause us to improve, but they can also be exhausting and overwhelming.

The four challenges that most programs face on a day-to-day basis are:

- Doing more with less: How can we develop and implement more new events and programs that will increase our customers without increasing staff or overhead costs?
- Increasing competition: How do we compete with local, national, and international competition without running our offerings at a cost that erodes our required operating margin?
- Need for information: How do we gather information about our customers so that we can better target them, as well as non-customers with similar profiles?
- Cost of doing business: How do we adjust our expense requirements or increase our prices in order to compensate for the continued increase in promotion, production, and administrative costs?

At the same time, we must be more responsive than ever before and we must be more focused on our customers. No longer are we managing products, but instead our responsibility is to manage customers. We must listen to what our customers need and want, and we must respond quickly.

Our organizations are customer driven and not staff driven. We are in a learning relationship with our customers. We are helping them get the learning they desire, while at the same time we are learning more about who they are while telling them more about who we are.

Because of this shift, there are six priorities that require our attention and focus. They are:

- Quality: Quality is now a given. In the past, we all strived to offer quality programs and events. Now quality is expected. If your organization does not offer quality events and/or programs, then the other five priorities are not even worth considering.

- Service: Service is another given. With the world focused on customer service and customization, our organizations are expected to be service-oriented and customer-focused. Customers want answers to their questions and they want their problems solved immediately.

- Speed: New products must be developed in a shorter time span. When we hear the customer has a need, we must be able to meet that need within days, or even hours of the request. We no longer just develop new courses or events in time for the next promotion, but instead we develop exactly what the customers want, when they want it, and we market it immediately. We cannot always wait for the next promotion.

- Innovation: Up to 30 percent of our products should be new each year. This requires that we are constantly evaluating our statistics and looking at trends. New products can be enhancements and/or spin-offs, but they need to be developed for our "star" customers. Retention is critical to our success. No longer can we be spending more and more dollars getting new customers. We must keep our old customers involved.

- Flexibility: Adults learn in many different ways. We must be flexible to their requirements. This requires us to look at presentation styles, location, and time. Adults want to make their own decisions about when, where, and how they will learn.
- Cost: Our events and programs must be affordable, not just for the customer but also for us. We must look at the competition, at what the market will bear, and also at what we can afford. On an average, we must be making our operating margin; if not, that means we must be eliminating the dogs and/or developing more new events and programs.

Handling Complaints

Complaints are never fun to handle. But they can be turned into good public relations and marketing for your program. In fact, complaints from learners are good for your program. They mean people care and there is something you can do to get them back again.

Some people even say to rejoice, not fret, when you get that nasty letter or complaint call. An *In Business* magazine survey found that companies that encourage their customers to complain about poor service and faulty products make more profits in the long run.

The study found that when dissatisfied customers successfully complained, they were more likely to remain loyal to the program and to tell their friends about the experience. Those who didn't or couldn't complain were more likely to stop using the program, service or product, and to spread their disdain by word of mouth.

In fact, while a satisfied customer may tell three other people about your program, some surveys indicate that a dissatisfied customer may tell as many as eleven other people. So it is well worth your time and energy to try to get that participant to support your program again.

Here's how. Listen to the customer's story without interrupting, then make a brief statement of empathy, says national consultant Francis Tritt.

"The person who is upset wants to know you have at least an understanding," Tritt says. "It doesn't necessarily mean an apology. For example, you can say. 'I'm really sorry you've had this problem.' The next step is to repeat the core of the complaint, ignoring the irrelevancies such as anger or exaggeration. Then you ask pertinent questions without being defensive or offering explanations. Customers don't care about your problems," says Tritt.

Finally, you take some kind of action. You make a suggestion; you give a choice or an option. If it's a referral to someone else, you explain why the referral is necessary. Simply saying "It's company policy" is never enough. If there is nothing left to do except say "no," then be apologetic. Indicate that you really wish "there was something we could do."

When citing your refund policy, state it as simply but positively as possible. If there are any options for the dissatisfied person, give him or her a choice, even if it doesn't seem like a choice. For example, "You could either sign up for another course this session, or wait until next session and use our credit voucher," appears to be giving the person a choice.

Explaining Your Program

How simply and quickly can you explain your program? Potential customers ask three questions regarding your basic activities:
1. What do you offer?
2. Who comes to your programs?
3. What are you about?

Being able to answer each of these questions in 25 words, without using organizational jargon, is important. Here are some tips for composing your replies:
- Be general, then specific. You want to be general enough in your reply to include any possible services to the person, but you also want to be specific enough to not seem vague. So begin with a general statement, but then follow it with some specifics or examples. More and more people are looking for

situations that apply to them, and stating that you serve everyone with every kind of program has less and less impact. For example, if someone asks you what your organization is all about, one could reply, "We try to meet the community's educational needs, and specifically we offer evening courses for personal enrichment, and some week-day seminars for business people."

- Write your responses down, memorize key phrases, and keep notes handy by the telephone if you need to. Using the proper word or phrase will achieve the results you want. Being fuzzy or using slang will create a poorer impression.
- Talk it over with the rest of the staff. Perhaps there is an overall statement or concise wording that is recommended to you.
- Practice it. Try writing out the answers to each of those three questions right now, and see if you can do it quickly and with fewer than twenty-five words for each answer.

Providing potential participants with concise and easy-to-understand answers to their basic questions about your program will make it easier for them to know about your operation and to become involved.

Chapter 16
Leadership

Leadership in the Internet Age

Many CEOs in lifelong learning leadership positions have been in the business for many years. The changes the Internet and globalization are requiring us to make are exciting but at the same time very challenging. The Internet is changing how we, as leaders, do program development, marketing, needs assessment, program management, and much more.

A new lifelong learning leader is beginning to evolve. A CEO in the Information Age is much different than a CEO in the Industrial Age. All business leaders are facing this shift. Lifelong learning is no different.

The following are key requirements of Information Age lifelong learning leaders.

1. CEO as Entrepreneur

An Information Age CEO must be an entrepreneur. This means a lifelong learning CEO must actively be looking for new opportunities. Opportunities may come in the form of new markets and/or new products. 50% of a CEO's time must be spent outside the office talking to customers and learning about what their customers want to learn about.

2. CEO as Change Agent

No longer can CEOs be focused on maintaining the status

quo. Change is important and must be constant. All staff must be continually looking at ways to increase the value of their customers' experience. CEOs must recognize the need to "educate" their employees and increase the intellectual capital of their organizations.

3. CEO as Lateral Leader

Running a lifelong learning program top-down is no longer possible. Staff must be given responsibilities and be made accountable. One person can no longer manage everything, and CEOs must delegate decision making to other staff members. Empowerment is important for both directors/managers and front line staff.

4. CEO as Brand Builder

Building your organization's brand is much more important than developing products. A CEO must concentrate a considerable amount of time building the program's brand. What makes your program more appealing than others? What are your organizational strengths? Why are you unique to your customers?

5. CEO as Customer Advocate

Customer retention is a key to success in the Information Age. Customers do not come back because of poor quality, poor service, or a lack of new products. CEOs must make sure quality, service and products are top notch and that staff members think customers first, organization second and themselves third.

6. CEO as Operations Specialist

Running a simple organization is important. All obstacles that complicate the running of the lifelong learning program must be eliminated. The delivery methods must be diversified but there must be a commonality between them all. Having the right tools, such as a web-based software system, is critical.

7. CEO as Coach

You are the leader of the team. You must set the example. Your team follows your lead. The first six points must be at the heart of your teaching and examples. If so, your team will grow your business and prosper individually.

If we want to survive as CEOs in the Information Age, we must change how we lead. Use these guidelines to help you plan how you will lead your lifelong learning program.

The New Rules In Lifelong Learning

The Internet has created an entirely new environment. The old rules don't work anymore. Only LERN has all of the New Rules and can help your organization succeed in the new century. First presented at the LERN Millennial Convention, here are the New Rules.

Rule 1. Shift from products to markets.
Only customer-driven organizations will survive and thrive in today's marketplace. Design your programs and activities around your audience. Find out their needs, then serve them. Stop creating programs, start responding to needs.

Rule 2. You have 7 primary market segments.
Twenty percent of your customers give you 80 percent of your income and surplus. We not only have to segment our audiences, we have to shift from trying to serve everyone to serving our best customers better.

Rule 3. Demographically code each customer.
In order to become customer-driven and remain relevant to your best customers, we need to input one demographic code (plus zip code) for each of our customers.

Rule 4. We have to be financially self-sufficient.
Only the LERN Financial Format will enable your organization to measure your financial success, improve your financial success,

and defend your budget. Operating Margins are key benchmarks for success in our industry.

Rule 5. Move from teaching to helping adults learn.

Self-directed learning will be the predominant learning theory and behavior for learners in the 21st century. Teachers need to move from teaching subjects to teaching learners.

Rule 6. The boundaries of geography, time and affiliation are gone.

Geography is no longer a boundary. The marketplace is now global. The objective now is to find your niche in the global marketplace.

Rule 7. Intellectual capital is your biggest asset.

Your Organizational Strength and USP (Unique Selling Proposition) are based on your people, including staff, teachers, participants and consultants.

Rule 8. The Internet will change how we learn.

The traditional lecture-style presentation has been shattered. Some 50 percent of all learning will be online. Cognitive learning will be done better online than in person. In-person teaching will totally change to discussion- and learner-oriented group sessions.

Rule 9. Move your whole organization to the Internet.

Your web site replaces your brochure. Registration is done over the Internet. Services and information are provided by your web site. Staff are supervised via an intranet. Vendors and suppliers are linked to your business intranet.

Rule 10. Cut costs.

Costs have to be cut, not covered. Increase Promotion, cut Production, lower total Direct Costs, boost Operating Margin, lower Administrative Costs, increase Net. Get rid of buildings and physical space. Get rid of supervision. Contract globally for the best.

Rule 11. Your institution has to play by the same rules.
Lifelong learning is central to our society for the 21st century. Your institution has to look and behave just like your lifelong learning unit. Your institution cannot ignore these rules and has to play by the same rules.

Transition Tools for the 21st Century

LERN has written a great deal about the transition from the Industrial Age to the Information Age. All lifelong learning organizations are experiencing this shift. Some programs are in the middle of the transition, while others are just starting the journey.

One part of the Information Age is online learning. Online learning, projected to be 50% of lifelong learning in the 21st century, is the "glamour component" of the Information Age. But it is not the only aspect of moving from the Industrial Age to the Information Age. As LERN has experienced and studied the shift, six "musts" have evolved. Any lifelong learning program retooling for the 21st century must think about and do the following if they want to be an Information Age organization.

1. We MUST perfect our operations.

The cost of making the shift to the Information Age is significant. Now more than ever, running your lifelong learning organization like a business is critical. The simplifying of the operations of your program is important for both staff and customers. The pace of running lifelong learning programs is dramatically increasing. Programs stuck in the world of meetings, process-laden decision-making requirements, top-down management (only the person at the top can make a decision), and meaningless reports will find it difficult to make the shift, may not ever leave the Industrial Age and thus will become a dinosaur and will soon be extinct.

Programs making the transition are doing the following:

A. Developing a web-based management system — a customized software system that runs on the Internet and manages all components of the program. This does not mean just online registration and online classes. Also included are database management collection and querying capabilities; course/event and promotion development; electronic confirmations and reminders; personalized "dashboards" (customer develop their own interest requirements that are immediately available to them on your web site); and financial and management reports that are key to operating lifelong learning programs.

B. Streamlining processes

LERN has outlined 15 lifelong learning processes, such as registration, program development, and refund management. Each of these processes must be redesigned. This probably means destroying your present process and implementing a new one that makes the customers' lives easier and adds value to their experience.

C. Contracting out instead of hiring

The less staff the more flexible a lifelong learning program can be. The more that can be contracted out, the easier it is for a lifelong learning program to change directions. Contracting out also allows you to work with the best and it saves you a great deal of money in training as well as staff management. Common tasks that are being contracted out are programming; promotion desk-topping, printing and distribution; management of computer labs; bookkeeping; and even registration.

D. Redesigning the organization's staffing structure

CEO/directors are focused on generating opportunities, managing the organization, and building intellectual capital. Programmers spend the majority of their time developing new courses/events and new programming directions. Operations people handle all of the day-to-day such as registration, finances, logistics, information generation, etc. Salespeople sell contract training and/or recruit students into high-dollar courses. A Promotions Professional manages the program's one-year market plan and does think marketing by analyzing demographic and purchasing information so that promotions can be more appropriately designed and targeted.

124

2. We MUST build long-term relationships.

More than ever before, you need to know who your customers are and what it takes to keep them happy. Your future hinges on your ability to improve your Repeat Rate, the percentage of participants who repeat from one year to the next. The benchmark percentage is 50%-70% and as we move into the 21st century, this percentage must increase. The cost of getting new customers is very expensive, so you need to be providing quality, service and new programs and learning opportunities.

Programs focused on improving their relationship with their customers are doing the following:

A. Monitoring their Repeat Rate

You need to know it. It is the most important benchmark you should be measuring your program up against. Included with Repeat Rate is Lifetime Value (LTV). By knowing your Repeat Rate and the average spent per course/event, you can project the lifetime value of each customer.

B. Targeted marketing

Lifelong learning programs are beginning to transition away from one comprehensive brochure/catalog/schedule, to multiple targeted promotions that support the interests of the program's segments. At the same time, web sites are being upgraded with pretests, additional information about the course/event and instructor, and "hooks" that get people to return and start using the web site as their main source of information.

C. A more global outreach

Your audience is no longer just your community or your membership. Your audience is anyone in the world who might have an interest in a product(s) you provide. Online learning is an obvious avenue, but so are conferences, seminars, institutes and other training opportunities that gather people together at your location or at easier-to-travel-to locations.

D. Showing you care

For most participants, the little extra special touches mean a great deal. An e-mail reminder about their upcoming class; an anniversary card thanking them for their years of participation; unexpected discounts; etc. are examples of what some programs are doing. Some programs provide membership options. Programs are also showing they care to their instructors and staff — the two other legs of the organization's triangle of participation.

3. We MUST build a significant brand.

You must know what your Unique Selling Proposition is, as well as your organizational strengths. What distinguishes you from your competition? This is not a product or a service, but instead the image your customers have of your organization. LERN's significant brand is *"Information That Works!"* Providers of lifelong learning come to LERN for practical, how-to information that helps them improve their program's performance. Why do your customers come to you and how do you build on the image and spread the image to more non-customers?

Programs dedicated to branding are doing the following:

A. Determining their USP

In conjunction with best customers, they are determining their organizational strengths and the voids their program fills. Once determined they are aggressively capitalizing on their USP in promotions, when answering the phone, and in conversation with customers and non-customers.

B. Everyone wears a marketing hat

In order to improve the image of your program, you need to make sure all staff and instructors are aware that they are part of the marketing effort. They may not develop promotions, a subset of marketing, but they do build the image of the organization by how they communicate with customers; the extra care they give to providing participants with a quality learning experience; the speed with which they respond to customer questions, complaints and requests; and the flexibility of program delivery.

4. We MUST ensure that channels of communication with customers are consistent.

The 21st century, the Information Age, is requiring us to expand our methods of communication to customers. No longer do we just produce a brochure/catalog/schedule, but now we have targeted promotions, a web site, partnerships, and many other creative ways of getting the word out. Consistency is now critical. The look needs to be the same, as well as the service provided. Each channel of communication must provide the same or more information (a web site can provide the same information as a brochure, but it can also provide more and certainly should not provide less).

When partnering to run a program (in conjunction with a local business or organization) or to advertise our programs (another web site), we must be very clear that this partnership does not delude or hurt the message we are trying to send to our customers and to the public.

A great deal of time has been put into building your brand, so you must be selective about whom you allow to have an opportunity to build or destroy that brand. Expanding channels of communication will only get more important in the 21st century, but good decisions need to be made about whom you expand with or how you expand.

5. We MUST make investments and utilize sound financial decision-making.

Surviving and thriving in the 21st century is very different from the late 20th century. The speed of business has grown dramatically and to compete, a lifelong learning program needs to think in terms of the future. This requires investing in the organization. Spending money now for future paybacks that can be hugely profitable. In the 20th century we were concerned about the profitability of each individual program, but in the 21st century we will be much more concerned about the profitability of the overall organization. This might even mean we lose money for a period of time in order to be positioned for success in the future.

Those programs investing in online learning today are doing so with an eye to the future. Capital and staff time are being allocated to a venture that hopefully in the future will provide significant income. If you are investing in a web-based management system, you know the cost is significant, but the long-term benefits to both staff and customers should outweigh the costs with reduced expenditures and increased income.

Programs investing for the future are doing the following:

A. Investments into research and development (developing online course capabilities) and building infrastructure (building a web-based management system) are being looked at as capital expenses (spread out over 3-5 years) instead of a cost allocated to that year's profit and loss statement. Research and development and infrastructure building are investments much like purchasing computer hardware for the office or building a new building.

B. Time and energy needs to be spent selecting how investment money should be spent.
Being financially prudent means an organization knows how much it can afford to spend on investment. This number will differ dramatically among lifelong learning programs, and the decision on what to spend will depend on the long-term payback, as well as the options for obtaining the money. The money may come from profits/reserves; from grants or allocations; or from partnerships. It is most important to be smart about where the money is spent. For some organizations that might mean online learning, while for others it might mean the development of a quality brochure or the improvement of classroom chairs.

C. Although the cost of investment is being spread out over 3-5 years, the yearly promotion, production and administrative expenses must meet anticipated benchmarks.
It is more important than ever to make sure that the product mix being provided is profitable. Promotion and production should not exceed 60% (you should be striving for 50%) of income and administrative expenses should not exceed 35%.

6. We MUST become a liaison that adds value, or find one to join.

All lifelong learning programs are struggling to make the public aware they exist. Some programs are much better known and positioned than others. Those programs are the ones in the best position to see faster growth. By using the first five points as guidelines, larger programs can quickly outdistance the pack and build their customer base. For many of them this will happen by partnering with other lifelong learning programs and/or acquiring them. If you are in Atlanta and want to have a presence in San Francisco, it is certainly most cost effective to partner or acquire instead of starting new.

For smaller programs, the question is whether they want to compete with the major players or if they want to find and exploit a niche market. Once again within the niche markets there will be the major and minor players. If you cannot anticipate 20% or more of the market share, you are a minor player. The successful major niche players will be looking to partner/acquire minor players or put them out of business.

Your lifelong learning program needs to figure out what kind of player it is. Once that is done, you need to decide what your future looks like. Will you be able to survive as is or should you be looking to partner. You might look to acquire or be acquired, or you might look to partner with a smaller or larger program.

Acquisition is not the norm in lifelong learning, but during the next five years we will see this start to happen. Programs that are losing money will look at ways to cut their losses and one way will be by selling their lifelong learning program to a local, national or global organization. Some programs will not sell, but will instead contract with another organization to run their program. Others will find a way to tie in with a larger program, possibly by just having them advertise specific courses/events the program has to offer but needs the larger player's promotional capabilities. In this scenario, the programs with the most active web sites will hold an advantage.

We are all trying to figure out what the 21st century will mean to lifelong learning programs. As we watch what is happening in the business world, we can see trends that lifelong learning will also have to confront. It is best to prepare now for a future that will require perfected operations; long-term relationships; branding; multiple channels of communication; investment capital; and value-adding liaisons.

Bibliography

Information for *Continuing Education: The Essentials* was taken from the following books, manuals and publications, published and available from LERN.

1. *Executive Leadership Institute Manual*, by Greg Marsello and William Draves

2. *The Marketing Manual* (Sixth Edition), by LERN professional staff and consultants

3. *The Financial Manual*, by LERN professional staff and consultants

4. *How to Teach Adults* (Third Edition), by William A. Draves

5. *The Free University: A Model for Lifelong Learning*, by William A. Draves, Follett Publishing Company, Chicago, 1980, forward by Malcolm Knowles

6. *The Successful Brochure Manual for Seminars and Conferences*, by Julie Coates and Paul Franklin

7. *The Successful Brochure Manual for Community Programs*, by Julie Coates and Paul Franklin

8. *Developing Successful New Programs*, by LERN professional staff and consultants

9. Certified Program Planner (CPP) Study Guide and Readings, Greg Marsello, editor

For information on these and other publications from LERN, go to *www.lern.org*.

Chapter 4 Notes

[1] J. Roby Kidd, *How Adults Learn* (New York, NY: Association Press, 1973, 1959), page 95

[2] Ronald Gross, *Invitation to Lifelong Learning*, (Chicago, IL: Follett Publishing Company, 1982), page 48

[3] Kidd, page 95

[4] Sharan Merriam and Rosemary Cafarella, *Learning in Adulthood* (San Francisco, CA: Jossey-Bass Publishers, 1991), page 307

[5] Laurent A. Daloz, *Effective Teaching and Mentoring* (San Francisco, CA: Jossey-Bass Publishers, 1986), page 157

[6] Russell Robinson, *Helping Adults Learn and Change* (Milwaukee, WI: Omnibook Company, 1979), page 50

About LERN

The Learning Resources Network (LERN) is the leading consulting organization in continuing education and the largest association in continuing education in the world.

Begun in 1974, LERN is a non-profit, tax-exempt education organization. Services are provided by 30 staff and consultants located across the United States and in other countries. Members serve in the LERN leadership, including the Board of Directors.

LERN's mission is to extend lifelong learning to all. We are the authoritative, distinctive source of practical information related to lifelong learning programs, such as continuing education programs. Our slogan is *"Information That Works!"*

At the time of this writing, LERN serves over 2,000 continuing education programs a year. More than 1,000 continuing education programs are Organizational Members and receive free and exclusive member services. Almost another 1,000 continuing education programs are customers every year, participating in LERN education and events, contracting with LERN for consulting or training, or otherwise purchasing products and services from LERN. Continuing education programs engaging LERN receive a 10:1 payback and ROI on all LERN services and consulting, with membership guaranteed.

LERN has the top consultants in the continuing education business, with professional staff and consultants specializing in various aspects of continuing education. Major areas of expertise include:

Continuing education training and consulting

Training, consulting, answers and solutions on eMarketing, marketing, promotion, finance, pricing, contract training, certificate programs, online courses, online certificates, program development, curriculum building, leadership, management, needs assessment, strategic planning and other advanced how-to aspects of continuing education.

Strategic planning

LERN also engages and works with institutional leaders and decision makers engaged in long-term institutional strategic planning and faculty development.

Online learning and faculty development

LERN is a leading provider of online faculty development, offering the Certified Online Instructor designation, online courses, and in-person faculty development seminars.

Vision

Strategies for organizational success in the 21st century, based on the heralded book *Nine Shift: Work, life and education in the 21st century*. Services include on-campus consulting, training and strategic planning workshops.

Research

LERN is a leading research organization in continuing education, higher education and learning, including pedagogy and teaching strategies.

Standards

LERN leaders are actively engaged in creating new educational standards for the 21st century, including the International Learning Unit (ILU), certificate standards, individual learning accounts, and other standards.

LERN Resources

Membership Benefits
- All six members receive benefits.
- All six receive our practical, how-to magazines.
- Free consulting via phone, mail, fax, or e-mail
- Annual brochure critique
- eLERN, your e-mail newsletter
- Access to the member-only area of *www.lern.org*

LERN Club
Members-only area of our web site at *www.lern.org*, featuring:
- 3,000 practical, how-to reports
- Monthly chats
- Consulting Suite
- Networking
- Membership directory
- Monthly news and trends

Publications
Books, manuals, publications, tapes and videos in 12 areas, including marketing, finance, program development, Internet and web, online courses, teaching, contract training, needs assessment, brochures, and more

Seminars
New topics are introduced every year. Seminars are offered at locations across the U.S. and Canada.

Conferences
- *Lifelong Learning Conference*, fall, "the most exciting week of the year in lifelong learning"
- *Teaching OntheNet*, spring, annual conference on online learning and teaching
- *Best Practices Conference*, spring, the latest information from the best experts

Institutes

Our four-day Institutes are the most intensive, advanced, comprehensive professional development available. Held in January/February and June. Also available in-house or on-site. Topics include:

- Program Management
- Contract Training
- Association Education
- Executive Leadership
- Successful Needs Assessment & Market Research
- Marketing
- Successful Certificate Programs
- Strategic Online Course Planning

Certified Program Planner (CPP)

The leading professional development recognition in lifelong learning. More than 1,000 CPPs awarded since the program started in 1990. Three specialties are offered:

- Standard CPP, focus on lifelong learning programming.
- Contract Training specialty.
- Certificate Programs specialty.

Program Review and Certification

The only review and certification especially for lifelong learning programs. A set of four essential criteria measure present performance. A second set of 46 performance criteria measure future success.

Consulting

On-site consulting is available from any of our LERN consultants. We match your needs with our consultants' specialties and expertise areas.

Training

LERN is constantly doing staff training and professional development for organizations. We can come to your organization and do training from one to four days in length on a variety of topics. We work with you to customize the program to your needs.

In-Houses

Your organization can sponsor a LERN seminar or Institute and promote it to other programs in your area, charging them a fee to attend. This is a cost-effective way to get the best professional development for your staff.

Teaching OntheNet

A curriculum of one-week online courses for teachers about teaching in the Internet Age. LERN is the leading online provider of professional development for faculty in higher education. Instructors are the foremost authorities and book authors. Courses include:

- Teaching Online
- Designing Online Instruction
- Creating Streaming Audio
- Generational Learning Styles
- Building Learning Communities in Cyberspace

Areas of Expertise

LERN is the foremost authority in the world in two areas: 1) lifelong learning; and 2) online learning. Our areas of expertise include:

Lifelong Learning
- Marketing
- Finance
- Needs assessment
- Brochures
- Registration
- Program development
- Market research
- Staffing
- Management
- Pricing

Online Learning
- Learning online
- Designing online instruction
- Creating successful discussions online
- Teaching online
- Creating streaming audio
- Developing online courses
- Marketing online courses
- Strategic planning for online courses